From Brainwave to Business

FT Prentice Hall
FINANCIAL TIMES

In an increasingly competitive world, we believe it's quality of thinking that gives you the edge – an idea that opens new doors, a technique that solves a problem, or an insight that simply makes sense of it all. The more you know, the smarter and faster you can go.

That's why we work with the best minds in business and finance to bring cutting-edge thinking and best learning practice to a global market.

Under a range of leading imprints, including *Financial Times Prentice Hall*, we create world-class print publications and electronic products bringing our readers knowledge, skills and understanding which can be applied whether studying or at work.

To find out more about Pearson Education publications, or tell us about the books you'd like to find, you can visit us at **www.pearsoned.co.uk**

From Brainwave to Business

How to turn your brilliant idea
into a successful start-up

Celia Gates

**Financial Times
Prentice Hall
is an imprint of**

Harlow, England • London • New York • Boston • San Francisco • Toronto • Sydney • Singapore • Hong Kong
Tokyo • Seoul • Taipei • New Delhi • Cape Town • Madrid • Mexico City • Amsterdam • Munich • Paris • Milan

PEARSON EDUCATION LIMITED

Edinburgh Gate
Harlow CM20 2JE
Tel: +44 (0)1279 623623
Fax: +44 (0)1279 431059
Website: www.pearsoned.co.uk

First published in Great Britain in 2010

ISBN: 978-0-273-74405-4

British Library Cataloguing-in-Publication Data
A catalogue record for this book is available from the British Library

Library of Congress Cataloging-in-Publication Data
Gates, Celia R. F.
   From brainwave to business : how to turn your brilliant idea into a
successful start-up / Celia Gates.
      p. cm.
   Includes index.
   ISBN 978-0-273-74405-4 (pbk.)
 1. New business enterprises. 2. Entrepreneurship. 3. New products.
4. Inventions. I. Title.
   HD62.5.G38 2010
   658.1'1--dc22
                                                    2010032830

ARP Impression 98

Typeset in 9/13pt ITC Stone Serif Std Medium by 3
Printed in Great Britain by Clays Ltd, St Ives plc

Contents

Acknowledgements

With special thanks to the Matriarchs, Mentors and Mates who have made me who I am and made it possible for me to share this information with you.

My grandmother and inspiration, and my long-suffering parents Rosemary and John Gates – thank you for enduring my exploits with such encouragement and support and for having the foresight to provide me with a valuable and balanced education.

The International School of Milan; St Felix School, Southwold; Loughborough University; Cardell Media and the Glazer-Kennedy Institute.

Kane Kramer, Chairman of the British Inventors Society and organiser of the British Invention Show, whose crash course in business by action provided me with the platform from which to progress. Bola Olabisi and the GWIIN network whose support, encouragement, friendship and passion empower me to pursue my dreams.

Annabel, my wonderful sister, who inspires me endlessly with her exploits of endurance (running coast to coast in 6 days and cycling from Lands End to John O'Groats in 3 days). My plethora of precious and lifelong friends for loving me as I am.

Thank you

Foreword

'If you are looking to understand how a good idea can become a profitable business then this book will help you get off to a great start.'

Every successful entrepreneur takes a different path to market. Some license their innovations to others to sell. Some sell their products to distributors. Still others work to develop a first-person relationship with the customers they serve. There is no one path to market for new ideas because there is no one definition of success. That means, to be successful, you must build your own path ... and the best way to do that is seeing the roads others have taken.

Celia R. F. Gates has written a book that takes a reader along her path from initial insight to successful distribution of her award-winning pans. Her insightful, sometimes poetic, prose describes what she has learned on a journey that started in her grandmother's kitchen and led to her receiving the British Consumer Invention of the Year award.

Every successful entrepreneur can point to turning points, decisions, strategies and suggestions that brought them closer to achieving their goals. By reading this book you learn how Celia manufactured her success right along with her award-winning pans. You will also learn where she stumbled, how she fell, and why she was able to pick herself back up again.

Celia uses her story to demonstrate the key elements common to every entrepreneurial success. She developed and packaged a great innovation; she researched and identified her customers and from that defined her market. She built a path to her customers and found a way to produce, manufacture and deliver her products to them at a price they can afford.

If you are an artist or designer, a creative individual or simply someone with a brilliant idea looking to understand how a good concept can become a profitable business, this book will help you get off to a great start.

Enjoy.

Doug Richard
School for Startups

Preface

'If I had read this book first I would have saved myself at least £94,000 in costly mistakes.'

The snow twinkled in the sun with a teasing wink, challenging and encouraging me to break its pure, untampered surface. A few leaves had fallen with the night winds and evidence of the slow, nocturnal movement of winter animals showed traces of life but otherwise that brilliant, blank canvas was untouched. Making my own mark on it was all just too tempting ...

... sure there were risks. The snow had fallen in a driving wind. Earlier that winter it had been exceptionally warm. A layer of snow had thawed, refrozen and now lay beneath the surface of the 40 centimetres of recent snow fall. Avalanches were an issue. How big an issue? We'd need to test it to find out.

I have always been a passionate skier and this is the mindset with which I approach most things I do. I dip my toe in, I use my head and I go for it. When I go for it, I jump in and commit. I have never been averse to risk but I do calculate the odds. It's necesssary if you truly intend to survive and thrive from your new challenge. It's not always great fun. Sometimes, it's bloody hard work.

If you've ever had a brilliant brainwave then you will know exactly what I mean. It feels like a vision. There is a sense of awe and amazement at the prospect and extent to which you and others could prosper. It's a life-changing moment that provides you with a real sense of positive purpose. The more you think about the idea the more it bores deeper into your head. The more you try to put it from your mind the more brilliant it becomes. It gives you a rush of excitement and keeps you awake into the small hours of the night. You simply can't stop this wave from reverberating around your brain and you know that you're on to a winner but, the question is: **What on earth do you do with your brainwave?**

It's with this question in mind that I have written this book. And the answer is: You turn it into a brilliant business, of course!

This is the book that I wanted to read when I first had my idea for the concept of clever cooking: 'Bend the pan, not the man ...'. It all seemed so screamingly obvious to me but the question remained: what on earth was I supposed to do next? I searched for a book like this but it didn't appear to exist, so I searched online and discovered mixed views I didn't always trust; I spoke to specialist advisors who often seemed to have less experience than me. I got stuck in and I learnt from my mistakes instead. Now I hope to have turned this knowledge and experience into a useful tool for you. The advice and guidance I offer is cheap at the price. It has cost me over £94,000 in expensive errors to acquire. I hope to save you from such pitfalls (and the time it takes to fall into them) by providing you with an overview and understanding of how best to turn your burning brainwave into a brilliant business. But, I must also warn you in advance; this book is not for the fainthearted. It comes from the trenches and I hold back no punches in the news I deliver.

Not that long ago I was a skier living in the French Alps; prior to that I studied Industrial Design at Loughborough University and somewhere in between I had a couple of design jobs in both of which I was pretty miserable.

My mother will tell you that as a child, I set my heart on becoming a designer. When I was 10, I would have told you I was going to be a wood carver but once I discovered CDT (Craft, Design & Technology) I was hooked. At the age of 12, I declared that I was going to design non-electrical cooking equipment when I was a grown-up and, stubborn to the core, that's exactly what I have done.

My father was working in Milan at the time I was born so I grew up influenced by the culture of the Italian people, who pride themselves on cooking, good food and the convivial sharing of both. I was also fortunate enough, as a child, to visit the Alessi factory – a design-led, fun and friendly producer of exquisite housewares products – and remember being fascinated by the speed and action, the colour and scale and the enchanting flow of mass production. Yes, I was hooked.

When I embarked on my career as a designer, I was fully prepared. Fully prepared to take over the world, that is. How was I going to do it? Well, let's just say that I did not have a clue.

Having had my 'light-bulb moment' sitting in my granny's kitchen as she prepared us both some lunch, I look back now and almost envy the blind confidence with which I proclaimed my personal mission. Oh, if only I had known then what I do now – I would have saved *so* much time, and even more money! How very much easier and safer my initial investment would have been if only I had known what I do now. I don't want you to make the same mistakes. Please, use this guide to reduce your own risks. It really is much safer and easier to turn your brainwave into a successful business when you take the time to acquire the necessary skills and properly plan your journey.

Making life safer and easier has also been my mission in the world of cookware. I've introduced a product that makes cooking safer and easier for everyone by saving you time and energy in the kitchen, thereby achieving a personal goal.

In doing so, I have come to realise many things. Ever-greater problems seem to be continually presenting themselves. It is now more necessary than ever for us all to begin to accept individual responsibility to improve the world in which we live. People like you and me – people, that is, who I assume to be driven to make a positive difference, committed to helping themselves rather than relying on others, dedicated even to helping others to improve their own situations – we need to stand up and take action.

My intentions here are to empower you to take action to turn your brainwave into a business. I intend to help you achieve your goals by providing you with the skills and foresight you need to start your business positively and purposefully. I also hope to spare you some of the horrors and hazards which you may encounter. I am not ashamed of the mistakes I have made – these have taught me swift and valuable lessons, but experience is not the only way to acquire knowledge, especially when knowing something in advance could save you thousands of pounds.

This is your 'how to guide' on turning your brilliant brainwave into a simply brilliant business.

I live and breathe the business of innovation and entrepreneurship. It is challenging and immensely rewarding. Bringing your idea to market or turning your brainwave into a brilliant business is also your personal journey. The better equipped and prepared you are, the more skills you can acquire quickly, the more likely you are to succeed and enjoy the ride.

As you read this innovative business start-up guide, you will be presented with various options which you can explore further by simply turning to the appropriate page. This book has been set out like a series of stepping stones so that you may find guidance that propels your progress. The information provided is not conclusive, it is provided to widen your horizons and prospects. Seek as much advice as you need, keep your own counsel and draw your own conclusions but above all believe in your own potential as you set out in pursuit of your dreams. Take action and work relentlessly to continually optimise your results. Enjoy your progress.

This is all about your adventure. If it is well planned out then it is going to be fun and it's going to be profitable too. Enjoy – and do let me know how you are getting on.

(www.FromBrainwaveToBusiness.com)

My story

How it all panned out for me

Pans!

Who would have thought that they would take over my life?

According to my mum, I did. Seemingly, I announced to her at the tender age of 12 that I was going to grow up to design non-electrical kitchen equipment!

I've always had an entrepreneurial character and began an early career in the daffodil business with my cousin Mary – a short-lived experience with a memorably unpleasant ending. We were seven years old at the time. Our parents and grandparents were not best pleased when their three-hour search ended with the discovery that the yellow clusters of daffodils decorating the driveway had disappeared whilst two young children clutched them by the roadside next to a sign saying '50p per bunch'. Needless to say, this was the start of it all. A quick lesson in negotiation from an entrepreneurial grandfather allowed our business to flourish, provided the supplier was paid 1p per piece of stock.

This was how life was set to continue. At school I made and sold jewellery and Christmas decorations – white geese being the speciality, if my memory serves me well. My university studies were largely subsidised by organising student ski trips from which I gained a healthy profit and a healthy holiday in the process. I funded a 'gap-year' in much the same way, managing part-time employment in between entrepreneurial pursuits.

And then, I started my 'proper job'. I was working as a designer in the field of my dreams and my lifelong ambitions were realised when, at the age of 23, I was promoted to the position of Design Manager of a fairly sizeable housewares company but … I felt disenchanted. I was bored and I was miserable and I hated the confines a 9–5 structure inflicted on my creativity. I couldn't get my head around the fact that I'd achieved what

I'd always dreamed of and now I hated it. It wasn't until I was offered a significant pay rise and an Audi TT that I ultimately realised why.

I didn't want to belong to the men in grey suits. I needed my own autonomy. I needed the opportunity to accept or decline, to set my own path and to travel at my own speed – my soul needs such freedom to this day. Becoming an entrepreneur was seemingly second nature but I was never told this and took a while to accept it as being a viable opportunity. What I did realise was that I needed to get out of my job. So, I packed everything into the back of a Peugeot 205 and returned to a place I had discovered during my year out.

The saucepan concept was burning in my head. I had presented the idea to my previous employers and was given the opportunity to develop some early designs but they were unsure of the concept and not convinced that it fitted in with their growth strategy or existing range. I, on the other hand, was adamant as to its potential. I had to understand the ergonomics fully and develop the design further. But I needed to think more about it first.

So I moved back to the place I loved: the enchanting mountain valley of Serre Chevalier where I spent four years hiding myself in the hills and conducting my research and design evaluation. And, the best thing about doing all this in a French ski resort is that most of my greatest friends were (and still are) amazingly talented chefs. What better way to test the designs!

I took part-time work in kitchens. I got as close to real, function chefs as employment laws allow and I set about understanding the problem. I got distracted along the way but gained valuable business experience running a hotel and bar, taking the tourist inter-seasons to further my research. I had tremendous fun, skied like a goddess, made huge progress on my designs and returned to the UK with a knowledge of ergonomics and handle design engineering second to none to present my findings at the British Invention Show in 2004. The response was outstanding and I was compelled to plough on.

This is where the action I took really started to kick in. And, where I shy away from my naiveté and chastise myself for the costly mistakes that I made – but, I didn't know how to proceed and nobody seemed able to tell me.

People were prepared to invest in me – for large stakes of equity. They were prepared to take control and cut me out of the equation. They were prepared to parade and ride on the back of my success but nobody seemed able to protect and advise me.

So, I protected myself and I took a massive risk. I sold a house I had bought in Leicester and invested this in starting my business. The bank match funded me and off I went. Off to Malaysia to spend fortunes on tools I would never use whilst my competitors readied themselves to prevent my product from ever seeing the light of day. It was heart breaking.

I'd positioned myself perfectly and was presented with any innovator's 'deal to die for' – a simultaneous global launch in 74 countries, accompanied by a six-figure royalty advance and 8% thereafter. But, as is so often the case, when something seems too good to be true then it usually is.

Thirteen agonizing months and a hideous stress rash later, I was in ruin. The business had been brought to its knees defending a series of unfounded writs guaranteed to dissuade any potential licensor from completing a deal which, needless to say, had fallen through. I was emotionally and physically at my wits' end. Deserted and isolated. Boy-friendless. The softly spoken, gently delivered suggestions from friends and family that 'now might be a good time to pack it all in' merely fuelled my frustrations.

I never stood for bullying at school and I was darned if I was going to give in to bullying in business. Staying true to myself and to my idea, I pursued my progress against the odds by finding reputable suppliers in the Far East and importing a controversial container of cookware which my competition threatened to have confiscated at customs.

Nobody had the right to try to stop me bringing my ideas to market and I was prepared to put these idle threats to the test, so I imported my first container and made myself proud in the process. I unloaded it with a lump in my throat and then took my long-suffering mother out to lunch.

Next came the job of selling the saucepans and I wish in hindsight that I'd planned this better beforehand. I learnt through trial and error, actively seeking mentors and mates with parallel projects, through whom I was able to accelerate my learning. Testing on a small scale to gauge a direct response from my audience – freezing to death on market stalls; getting soaked to the skin at country fairs; stumbling nervously, suited and booted through the doors of the buyers prepared to open them marginally enough for me to squeeze through – I made progress. It worked and I got results.

The people who were buying my products were pleased. I began receiving letters thanking me for the design, explaining what a difference it made to their lives and asking what other products were soon to be available.

I started to design on demand, according to my customers' needs, and to scale up the levels of production. I was buzzing around like a blue-arsed fly, taking so much action that the magnetic fields around me were literally drawing more customers towards me. I was focused and I was determined and I was starting to see the positive effects.

My British Consumer Invention of the Year award was superseded by the prestigious title of European Female Designer of the Year which followed an invitation to Berlin to receive special recognition from the European Community for my contribution to innovation. The product opportunities were flying in thick and fast and the process of licensing the rights to a UK-based distributor was a delightful experience lasting three weeks.

Now, I've surprised myself by writing the book I wished I'd read when I first started out. I hope you find that it helps you.

The truth is your real-life knowledge will come from firsthand experience. We all make mistakes; it's what we do with them that counts!

Good luck with turning your brainwave into an absolutely brilliant business. Please share your experiences with others and join me and many more people like you on our website and in our forums.

As an owner of this book you are also entitled to attend one of my seminars absolutely free of charge. Visit the website at www.FromBrainwaveToBusiness.com to find out when the next one will be held.

I've shared my story, now I am looking forward to getting to know you better and watching your ideas blossom into brilliant businesses.

All the best

Celia Gates
European Female Designer of the Year 2007

An ode to the unknown path

Weirdos in garden sheds,
beards full of yesterday's dinner,
BO patches
and charity shop ties.
What you've heard about inventors –
it's lies, lies, lies.
What you've heard about business
is stories of success
and people who lie
to cover their mess.
What we know of success
sounds just fine.
It's all about yachts
and drinking good wine.
Of the path of how to get there,
little is known.
The few who travel it
do so, alone.

Celia Gates – July 2008

Introduction – Get set and go!

Having an idea

Let's start from the very beginning: the birth of your new idea. If you've had a moment of genius, a flash of inspiration or the wave of alternative reality commonly called a brainwave, then this is a huge compliment to you. If, like millions of people, you're still slightly baffled by the belief that you too could have an original and brilliant thought, believe me, yes you can and you've come to the right place. Just keep reading.

> **if you've had a moment of genius, a flash of inspiration then this is a huge compliment to you**

Anyone and everyone is capable of having a 'light-bulb moment'. Anyone and everyone is capable of turning this brilliant brainwave into a stunningly successful reality too. The problem is: **where on earth do you begin?**

Here is a good start: acquire knowledge and then take action. Often when we don't take action it is simply because we are unsure of what action to take. Don't beat yourself up about procrastination, simply spend time finding out more about the type of expedition – that is to say, the type of business adventure – that you are embarking on. This guide will give you an overview of your journey but I want you to start out knowing what you are getting into.

> **acquire knowledge and then take action**

As an often-quoted, general rule of thumb, you will find that, out of 33,000 ideas, only 3,000 ever get written down; 300 are developed further; 30 get to the stage of considering intellectual property and three are filed for official ownership. **Only one idea becomes a reality.** The odds of turning your idea into a success are not in your favour.

This horrifying fact, however, has almost nothing to do with the initial quality of your idea and nearly everything to do with what you, as the owner of your idea, decide to do with it next. In short, your success in this business or game all boils down to *you*. The decisions you make, the actions you take – you – are ultimately responsible for the success of your brainwave as a business or enterprise. How you set about turning this concept into a reality has everything to do with the attitude you adopt from the outset. You will acquire the skills you need along the way.

> ❝ your success in this business or game all boils down to you ❞

In picking up this book you have already demonstrated that you have the right attitude. You are obviously serious about developing your ideas and you are prepared to take action to find out more about how best to set and achieve your goals. Let's start by stopping you from immediately becoming another failed statistic.

If you are ready to see your brainwave blossom into life, if you are waiting with a watering mouth for the taste of success, if you know deep down that, against the odds, you are one of the successful few that will make it, then take action to reduce your odds of failure today. **Write your idea down**. Keep this book as your guide and reference manual. Use it as your own map and route-finder. Plan your route and chart your progress. Start getting into the habit of dating these and writing down any other thoughts that you may have along the way.

Securing copyright

Writing down your ideas could become critical to establishing your rightful ownership of the origination of your idea. You will start to accumulate chronological documented evidence of your idea's evolution which could, if necessary, be used to support claims over your rightful ownership. Protecting your ideas is paramount if you intend to profit and prosper from them. Start claiming unregistered rights over your ideas today by spending 5 minutes scribbling them down. By doing so, you will instantly improve your statistical chances of success and the unregistered copyrights could be valid for as long as 100 years after your death. You will also start to formulate your thoughts more clearly and be able to measure your progress more accurately. Don't think about it, do it! For the sake of 5 minutes, a few notes and a quick sketch ... can you really afford not to be writing your ideas down?

Moving forward

If you've not yet had an original thought or a burning brainwave, then don't worry. Over the next few pages we will look at what you can do to stimulate and accelerate new, innovative and original thoughts. We will get your creative juices flowing by opening up hidden gateways in your mind that allow you to think freely and challenge relentlessly. You will be equipped to judge and measure the potential for profits, prosperity and positive progress in all of your thoughts and actions and you will be encouraged to dream on a bigger scale than you ever believed possible. As your thoughts and ambitions expand, write them down.

It is not important how well defined your idea is; that will come with progress. You may have developed a working prototype and be ready for launch; you may have secured your intellectual property and be looking for manufacturing partners or investment; you may be selling millions in the market already or you may simply have a frail figment of a thought resting on the tip of your tongue. Keep quiet. Tell nobody your trade secrets. Write them down and secure their ownership, then decide what action is going to best propel your progress.

❝ get into the habit of thinking with a pen and paper in your hand ❞

Take responsibility. This is your idea. Fill out the box with a quick sketch, a few notes, an outline or a doodle of your brainwave and be sure to complete the copyright section too. This could be vital to your future. Seeing an idea written down helps you to focus your thoughts and, if you're not doing so already, you really must get into the habit of thinking with a pen and paper in your hand. **Write your thoughts down.** Not only will this help you formulate your ideas more clearly and provide further proof that you are the original developer but it will also give you a benchmark against which you can measure your progress.

Remember, the success of your idea ultimately boils down to you. You are going to quickly be acquiring new skills, travelling into uncharted

❝ there is always a way forward and this guide is here to help you find it ❞

territory, taking yourself way outside your comfort zone and, of course, you are going to reap the rewards. As with any journey, there will be highs and lows, moments of incredible elation and moments when you feel you can't go on. It is at times like these that you should take stock and look back at what you

Today's date.........../........./20..........

AN OUTLINE OF MY IDEA

have achieved. There is always a way forward and this guide is here to help you find it.

Bringing an idea to market can be a lonely occupation and in the early days you will need to become your own judge and jury. You will need to be able to measure your progress so that you can reward yourself accordingly because there is absolutely no doubt that to get to where you want to go will need a lot of grit and determination.

So this book should be treated like any other route-finder. Carry it with you on your journey. Read ahead to discover your destination and then work out the fastest and easiest route to take you there. Draw lines and highlight points of interest. Mark these with dates, thoughts and comments on your expectations. Refer back to these and amend them as the actual terrain you cover becomes clearer. Look, find out more and learn by testing first.

---

signposts to success

This is your adventure.

Choose the path that best suits your needs and the needs of your idea. At the end of each chapter you will be presented with a series of options allowing you to explore new areas, acquire further skills and make an informed choice – these are intended as signposts to your success. Read as many of them as you like. It's much less costly to experiment on paper than it is in real life and the more you know the more options you will find available to you.

As I said, enjoy the ride!

- If you don't yet have an idea or brainwave but would like to know how to generate one – turn to page 6.
- If you have an idea but you haven't got a clue what it's worth – turn to page 16.
- If you know your idea is brilliant but really don't know what to do next – turn to page 26.
- If you've secured your intellectual property and now want to take your invention to market – turn to page 81.
- If your idea is in the market but you're seemingly not making any money from it – turn to page 112.
- If somebody has stolen your idea and you need help – turn to page 135.
- If your business is going well and you're looking for new inspiration – turn to page 146.

How to generate new ideas

Stimulating your thoughts

New ideas have always come easily to me and I know that it's the same for many creative people. Coming up with new ideas is the fun part, where you give your mind free rein and explore uncharted ground. It's the part where, in an instant, you can enter a whole new realm of opportunity which nobody has ever seen before. **It's an amazing feeling – that EUREKA moment**. Suddenly, it's as if your thoughts become crystal clear – the light switches on somewhere up in your head and bingo! you know that you are on to a winner.

I know not everybody finds it easy – but trust me when I tell you: you can find it easy too. The principles and techniques are easy to teach and easy to learn. By spending time acquiring these simple skills and putting them into practice, you can overcome huge hurdles in a very short space of time. All you need to do is be prepared to retain an open mind. If you are still sceptical then relax and read on. New ideas will come to you when you least expect them to. You've just got to become consciously aware of how this happens.

If you are anything like the individuals I have met who claim not to be able to think like that then you need to know that inventors, innovators, creators of original thoughts and new concepts come from all sorts of different and varied walks of life. They are real people who have used their imagination, set their ambitions and followed their dreams. James Dyson was a student at the Royal College of Art before he began his career as an innovative entrepreneur. Trevor Baylis, the inventor of the clockwork radio, began his career as a technician in a Soil Mechanics lab; he later worked as a physical training instructor before applying his creative talents to developing a life-saving idea. Creative entrepreneurs come from all walks of life: parents, teachers, civil servants, professionals, people who are out of work, individuals looking to invest their money, craftsmen and women, computer whizz kids, mathematicians, musicians, chefs and shoemakers.

Anything and everything can be made possible when you begin to understand how. If you are one of the lucky ones who already understand that giving birth to a new idea is not only relatively easy but also enormous fun then this next insight might amuse you: people who struggle to come up with a new idea are usually looking in all the wrong places. They are *looking* for an idea in the first place – searching for them, seemingly – and herein lies the problem: a new idea cannot simply be found! Since a new idea does not exist how can you realistically think of finding it? You can search for it high and low if you like, but if it's not there then you can't possibly find it.

And, that is the whole point. When you create something new, you have an original thought. You give birth to a concept that has never occurred to anybody else before. It's new to you and it's new to the rest of the world. This makes it completely unique. Because of you, something that was not there before now exists. So, if you are currently looking for a new idea, be aware that new ideas simply don't exist. If you do find one, then the chances are that it belongs to somebody else. Know that it is not your original idea and be prepared to negotiate rights of reproduction with the rightful owner. If you want to come up with your own, unique idea then you need to be prepared to **generate** it.

> **" if you want to come up with your own, unique idea then you need to be prepared to generate it "**

Generating ideas involves stimulating your thoughts. Your thoughts function most creatively somewhere between a state of calm tranquillity and maximum alert, whereby the right-hand side of your brain – the side that deals with rhythm, rhyme and creativity – is being used in equal collaboration with the left-hand side of your brain – the side that deals with logic and reason. Such a situation could arise when you are out for a country walk and perhaps find yourself fiddling to release an unusual latch on a gate. You are relaxed, yet you are alert and you are faced with a logical problem in a creative environment.

Newton, as the story goes, was sitting under a tree watching the clouds go by when an apple dropped on his head, leading to his theory of gravity. He was relaxed and alert, thinking logically and creatively, at the time he had his light bulb moment. At the time I had my light bulb moment I was sitting in my grandmother's kitchen, chatting while she prepared lunch. I was relaxed, I was alert and I was **thinking logically and creatively**. We are all capable of thinking in this way and indeed we do so daily.

The fundamental difference between people who call themselves creatives and those who believe they are not capable of generating a new idea is their ability to take action. So, please don't take offence when I tell it as it is. If you are struggling to come up with a new idea then this is because you have adopted a lazy mindset. You are simply not using your brain extensively enough. In all likelihood **you are surrounded by fuel for new ideas** but you are probably not even aware of it and you are not using your potential to generate an original thought as a result.

❝ quite simply, to generate new ideas you've got to go looking for problems ❞

I've already mentioned the need to generate new ideas instead of looking for them. Well, a generator needs some sort of fuel or energy to power it and the fuel for generating ideas can be found in problems. Quite simply, to generate new ideas you've got to go looking for problems.

Looking for problems

Find problems and generate new ideas as solutions

Problems are easy to find. You encounter them every day. What you really need to look for is big problems: problems that affect lots of people; problems that cause world damage; problems that cost money or lives; problems in your life or the lives of those around you; problems within your business and so on ...

Whatever sort of problems you decide to go looking for, you need to take action to become consciously aware of them. For instance, next time you are relaxing in the bath and the soap falls into the water and you find yourself having to search around under the bubbles until you find it – note this as a problem. Instead of thinking 'Blast! Where's the soap gone?', think 'Ah HA – another problem!' and get your grey matter working.

Start collecting problems. They're everywhere. If you work in a hospital, you will be surrounded by problems; if you work in an office, it will be the same. If you are looking after young children or older relatives, then you will know all about the problems so many of us face every day. Look for problems that recur, problems that affect lots of people, problems that interest you and problems that are of growing concern.

There is no shame in deciding to take action to solve a specific problem because this benefits you. So much the better if you stand to gain from it. If it benefits you, then the chances are it is going to benefit countless other people too. Wheeling a shopping trolley through a busy supermarket, unloading your bags into your car; the fact that the house keys are always at the bottom of your bag or that your mobile phone always seems to ring just as you've got your hands full ... the list of problems goes on and on and solving them all is simply never-ending. Start looking out for problems that affect you or those around you and then choose which one you wish to pursue. If you are unsure, **pursue more than one problem**. By testing different solutions, you will soon know which problem has the potential to produce the simplest, most effective and profitable solution. Read the section on testing and optimising to find out more.

So start by finding out more about each problem.

Research and understand as much as you can

Experience the problem yourself; find out how other people are affected by this problem, and what they do to overcome it. Discover why it occurs and how frequently this happens. How many people does this problem affect? What are the consequences if the problem is not addressed? What solutions are currently being offered to the problem? What work is already being done? Is anyone else working on a similar solution to your own?

Often great minds do think alike. Climate, culture and conditions often cause innovative ideas to surface simultaneously. It is very important that you are aware of this from the start. If you are going to be in a race to patent your ideas then you might think differently about how you approach your goal. You also want to avoid spending years developing a 'new idea' that has already been protected, so conducting thorough research is crucial to saving you time and money in the long run.

Establish whether any patents for similar solutions to your problem have been filed already. You can do this by searching the large databases of patents that exist. If you are in or around London, then the British Library has a fantastic and free service to support you when you search existing patent files. In Cardiff, the Welsh Innovation Network provides similar support. Google also offers a specific patent search engine and each

Fifteen questions you should seek to answer when researching the problem:

1. What causes this problem?
2. Who is affected by the problem primarily?
3. How many people does the problem affect?
4. When and where does it occur?
5. How often does it occur?
6. Why does this problem exist?
7. What is the history?
8. What are the consequences of the problem?
9. What does the future hold?
10. How much does the problem cost (and to who)?
11. What does it feel like to suffer from the problem?
12. Who else is researching the problem?
13. Who is campaigning for a solution to the problem?
14. What current solutions already exist?
15. How urgently is there a need for a definitive answer?

individual patent office usually offers a database search system on their website. Spend the time necessary for a thorough search of existing intellectual property or pay a professional patent agent or intellectual property lawyer to do this on your behalf. Not only will you learn a lot from the process but you will instantly know how to avoid infringing ideas that have already been protected.

Use the internet to research your problem. Enter key words about your problem into a search engine and see what appears. Use keyword search tools to check the frequency with which other people express concern or seek solutions to your problem; post questions on forums; talk to specialist bloggers and find out what others are saying. Ask experts and interview regular sufferers; test and measure your results and then stand back from your findings and take a look at the bigger picture.

Once you have fully understood the problem, you can begin the process of unravelling it. By breaking the problem down into its simplest form and understanding every element of its causes and effects you will find yourself with a clearer understanding of what needs to be developed in order to provide a viable and innovative solution.

This is how to generate new ideas.

Brainstorming

Brainstorming is a brilliant way of pushing the boundaries of a problem. Be wary of making lists or thinking too logically. A list is a good way to break a complicated process into manageable tasks but it doesn't always help to expand the thought process. I actually find that lined paper stops me thinking straight! A blank sheet of paper offers no preconceived limitations and you are free to explore your thoughts to the limits of your imagination.

Create a brainstorming environment that is relaxed and allows the brain to be highly alert. In other words, be sure of the right lighting (natural daylight works best for me); make sure that there is no disruptive noise, interference, or distractions; be sure that it feels safe so that you are able to relax fully whilst remaining acutely alert. Then start thinking logically and creatively simultaneously. **You'll be amazed by some of the radical thoughts you start to generate.**

“ brainstorming is a brilliant way of pushing the boundaries of a problem ”

Mind maps

Take a large sheet of blank paper and start with one objective in mind. Write this in the middle of the page. Personally, I like to put a ring around it as this helps it to stand out as the page becomes more crowded. You will no doubt quickly develop your own style.

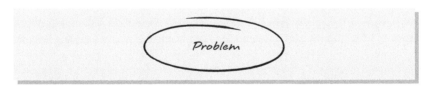

Then think about all the things that immediately spring to mind when you consider this central objective and draw arrows or lines to connect your thoughts as they occur.

This form of written thought processing is often called mind-mapping and it is an excellent way to explore and record your train of thoughts.

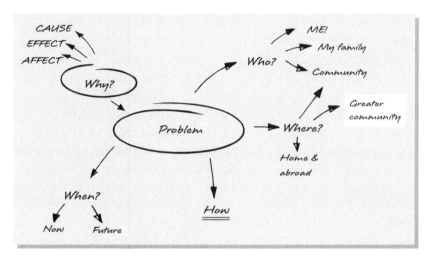

As you reach a pause in free-flowing thought, go back and read over some of the things that you have already written down. Consider each of these objectively, critically and constructively. New and further thoughts will come to you. Add and connect these to the bigger map and keep expanding and elaborating on what you have thought about before. Connect these thoughts with lines and arrows. Highlight words that are important, look for patterns and recurring words that need further attention. You might choose to use different coloured pens, or draw small pictures and diagrams to attract your attention back to areas of specific interest. Stronger lines, underlining and using capital letters can all be great ways of drawing emphasis to specific areas.

At each pause, sit back and study the bigger picture. Pin it to your wall if you like and use it as a benchmark for further inspiration.

A mind map can be as boggling and fascinating as you choose to make it. Simply select your subject and get thinking.

 Always finish a mind-mapping session with an action list of what you intend to do next. Having written your action list, circle the three principal activities on it. These are the three tasks that are fundamental to the progress of your idea. Concentrate on making these three things happen.

Take action

The more action you take, the more momentum you create; the more momentum you create the more your ideas and business will start to flourish and evolve. It sounds too simple, doesn't it?

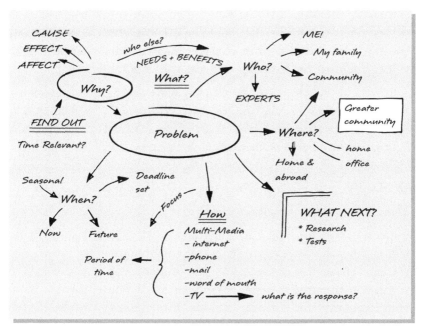

There are two reasons why we make it hard for ourselves: we procrastinate, we make excuses, we overcomplicate the situation and prevent ourselves from taking the very necessary action needed to generate ideas or power success. In doing so, we automatically paralyse our progress. Firstly, we make it hard for ourselves to take action because we are not sure what action to take. Secondly, we are scared of the consequences of action. Both of these factors freeze our ability to take action and it is imperative that you resolve today to overcome these mental blocks and continue to take positive action towards your success.

> **the key to becoming successful is taking action – consistent and continual action**

Quite simply, the key to becoming successful is taking **action** – consistent and continual action. Take multidimensional, calculated and accurate action. Measure your action, align your action with your intention and start building momentum. Use momentum to create strong magnetic fields of attraction and allow success to be drawn towards you.

Commit to generating new ideas by taking action to identify and understand problems. As soon as you understand the problem, your course of action will become clear and your concern over the consequences more calculated and less daunting. Whenever you find yourself stuck or struck still by a new challenge, step back to the original problem. Use your records and refer back to your mind maps to help you. Test and evaluate your progress. Armed with more skills, knowledge and fresh ideas, you will find yourself better equipped to make faster progress.

If you monitor your progress by keeping dated records of your thoughts, this will help you measure and improve your progress. You will become more adept at taking corrective action and more focused in your direction. Your progress will gain momentum as you gain confidence in your ideas.

Confidentiality

Remember to keep your ideas secret.

This can sound a little dramatic and of course you have the right to decide who you choose to trust. It all depends how much time, energy and resources you are prepared to commit to your project and how concerned you are about losing this original investment. If you tell anyone about your ideas, you are in danger of losing them and of jeopardising your chances of filing official intellectual property. A patent that contains information that has already been published or is already in the public domain will not be accepted as original. Don't risk ruining a friendship by disclosing confidential information. This is not about who you can trust, it is about protecting your ideas.

> **remember to keep your ideas secret**

If you do need to discuss your idea with anyone else (two heads are better than one, after all) then be sure to do so under the confines of a confidentiality agreement. This is a legally binding contract of secrecy between you and the person you wish to share your secrets with. If you are brainstorming together, be sure to agree in writing how you will deal with any original thoughts that emerge as a result of your combined discussions. It is perfectly acceptable for a consultant or brainstorming partner to accept that any new ideas that emerge from your conversation automatically belong to you. You need to be clear about the terms under which you are working. I would suggest that, in this instance, you should try to take into consideration your brainstorming partner's time rather than the value of his or her influence over your ideas as this will give you a less hindered route forward in the future.

The eureka moment doesn't always occur in an instant and often in the early days it is impossible to determine what your idea is actually worth.

When you do suddenly have a brilliant brainwave, record it, store it and then automatically assume the worst. Assume that you have jumped to the wrong conclusion. Challenge your idea in every way you can. What problem does it solve? How and why does it solve it? Consider the concept in reverse – break it back down into problems and ask yourself why, if it is really that simple, nobody has thought about it before. Only careful testing, research, development and constant optimisation will ultimately lead you to becoming a remarkable creator and an innovative and successful entrepreneur.

---

signposts to success

■ If you're still undecided about **taking your idea forward** then consider how much it could be worth to you in the future – turn to page 81.

■ If you would like to know more about how to **develop your idea** further – turn to page 26.

■ If you think you've generated an amazing idea and want to **secure your intellectual property** – turn to page 36.

■ If you would like to know more about **how you can make money from your ideas** – turn to page 81.

What to do with a brilliant brainwave

Quite simply, you've got to do something with a brilliant brainwave. Either that, or you've got to be prepared to live with constantly wondering what would have happened if you had done something with it! So, don't waste time. Take action. **Remember:** taking consistent and continual action is the key to business success.

Start with an understanding of how much you believe your potential idea to be worth and how much you are prepared to invest in making it happen. Remember, this is as much about you as it is about your ideas. An idea in your head is not worth very much. Written down on paper it is barely worth more. File for intellectual property and you start to add value to your brainwave but the real proof of the value of your idea will emerge only when you are selling consistently and continually to a growing group of loyal customers. Only then will you really be able to prove how much your idea is worth. Until then, it's educated guesswork.

If you are going to be committing considerable time, effort and resources to the development of your brainwave then it is imperative that you establish a basis from which to form an educated estimate of the potential return your early investment could bring. Is developing your idea going to be worth all the effort?

Estimating how much your idea is worth

Use the facts and figures that you have uncovered in your research to estimate the value of your idea. Being able to answer all of the following questions with substantiated facts will dramatically enhance your strength and position in the long run. It is worth doing your homework properly at this stage as a lack of solid research is one of the most common failings of a small start-up.

1. Who is going to benefit from your idea?

The more people who stand to benefit from your idea the more your idea has the potential to be worth.

When I first came up with the concept for an ergonomic saucepan handle – the product I now market under the Doctor Cook™ brand – I knew that my granny was going to benefit instantly. I knew too that I struggled to lift a hot and heavy saucepan from time to time and therefore I was going to benefit as well. I also knew that every household in the country owned at least three pieces of cookware and that carpal tunnel syndrome, repetitive strain injury and arthritis were growing concerns, affecting over 68% of the western world at some point during their lifetimes. I knew that my idea had the potential to benefit a lot of different people and this is what made the prospect of developing the concept so appealing.

❝ start with what you know and not just what you believe to be true. Do your research ❞

Remember: Start with what you know and not just what you believe to be true. Do your research and find out actual statistics. Work with real and current numbers. If you can break this down into categories or groups of people prioritised in the order in which they are likely to respond, this will help you focus the delivery of your marketing message as your business grows.

- How many people in your neighbourhood would benefit?
- How many people in your home town?
- In the country?
- In the world?

Avoid sweeping statements such as: 'Everybody in the entire world is going to benefit.' If indeed this is the case, then good luck but, for the purpose of the book, let's keep it realistic and consider **who is going to benefit the most** from your new idea.

If your idea is actually so specialist that it will really only benefit three or four people worldwide, you need to think about whether it is worth your while developing an idea exclusively for such a restricted audience.

If, on the other hand, you believe that every single person in the whole world is going to benefit instantly and therefore go rushing out to buy your brand-new idea then you need to consider which niche sector will respond first and what the size of this group realistically is.

Be honest with yourself. If anything, round numbers down (not up); be conservative with your estimates and do your research. There is absolutely no point in making statistics up. You are only lulling yourself into a false sense of security and this will not be to your advantage later on.

If you would like further help researching your target market then visit our website where you can download a set of very useful research tools for free simply by entering the barcode on this book. Visit www.FromBrainwaveToBusiness.com to receive these.

Once you have clearly identified who it is that you are trying to reach or target, the next step is to identify how best to reach these individuals and how easy it will be to do so.

2. How accessible is your target market?

How can you get hold of your target market? Do you have their contact details? Do you know them personally? Are they members of an organisation or club? Are they in the phone book or in a network online? Where do they currently purchase products or services which may be similar to your own? How difficult is it going to be to let them know about the idea you are currently bringing to market?

If you already have a long list of individuals who fall into the category of your target market and a positive, live relationship with them then accessing them and telling them about your idea is going to be easy. In this instance, the value of your idea will dramatically increase – not least if the list of individuals referred to is actually a list of customers who have already purchased something from you in the recent past. This is a highly valuable asset and estimating what percentage of these individuals are likely to invest in your latest idea will give you a clear indication of the current value of your idea.

However, you might find yourself in a situation where you are starting a new business and don't yet have any customers or lists of people who fall into the scope of your target market. You are still going to need to decide if it is going to be worth your while building such a list. Building anything costs time and money. Building a prototype, building a business or simply building a list of customers and potential leads is going to require a commitment of time and resources. The purpose of putting an estimated value on your idea is to help you decide whether or not it is worth investing in your concept.

Consider how accessible your target market is and how much it is going to cost you to reach them.

Next, it is vital that you understand what barriers, adversaries or boundaries you are likely to encounter.

3. Who or what are you going to be competing against?

Now you might think that, because this is a brand new concept that nobody has done before, you have no competition – and you'd be right, to a certain extent. But try to be a little bit more objective. Every industry has its giants and leaders, people who might consider it in their interest to make your life a misery and prevent your project from coming to market. We often hear of such stories in the software business and this is certainly something which has not been unfamiliar to me.

If you believe that there is considerable money to be made from your idea, then the chances are somebody else will already be trying to make this money for themselves. It is your job to convince consumers to invest their hard-earned cash in your product or service and this can often mean taking an existing market share away from somebody else.

You need to ask yourself:

- What do other people currently do to overcome the problems that my invention solves and where or how do they achieve this?
- What other brands or companies are operating in the industry I am trying to enter? What other products or services exist that do a similar job?

❝ never underestimate the power of your competition ❞

Never underestimate the power of your competition. They will go out of their way to protect their market share. You need to be aware of who they are and what they are currently doing to gain customers. Only then can you identify how you are going to gain your advantage.

4. What is your competitive edge?

Clearly identify your competitive edge. This is your point of difference, your unique selling points or the competitive advantage you have over the existing market. Ask yourself:

- What is it that makes me better than all the rest? Why is my idea or concept so much better?
- What is going to make my target market choose my ideas over and above any other options?
- What am I going to do that is going to make me stand out from the crowd and get noticed by the people you are appealing to?
- What is going to attract them to me?

If your only answer to this last question is price – 'My option is the cheapest!' – then I would ask you to think seriously about what added value you can offer your market.

❝ clearly identify your competitive edge ❞

Price is the weakest competitive edge of all. Your competitors will soon catch up with you on price and you cannot protect price with intellectual property. If you're starting off as the cheapest then what are you going to do when this is no longer the case? Price is a considered advantage, especially in the current economic climate, but it is not a strong competitive edge.

Think laterally and creatively. Add value to your concept by increasing the features and benefits that you are offering your customers. Find out what it is that they value most and refine your competitive edge in line with the needs and desires of your primary target market.

5. How sure are you of being the original creator of your idea?

As has already been mentioned, there is a real tendency for original ideas to emerge independently yet simultaneously. A shift in climate or culture, the introduction of new technology or production techniques, a new fashion or trend, the increased recurrence and reduced tolerance of a particular problem, often stimulate similar thought processes in different individuals. You need to be aware of the fact that you might not be the only person working on your ideas.

Consider how quickly you can move and how imperative it is that you are the leader and the first to market. This is why it is so important to do your background research. It would be devastating to see somebody else making a small fortune from your brainchild simply because you didn't take enough action efficiently enough.

Get moving fast … before somebody else does! Decide if your idea is really worth developing and then go for it.

If you are in a race against time then consider this a positive. The market is ripe for your brainwave and business concept right now. You need to get on the crest of that wave and ride it.

However, if, like many visionary people, you are actually ahead of the market – in other words, your idea is just too futuristic for mainstream adopters to immediately embrace – then spend the time better educating and understanding your market as you prepare your launch strategy.

This is what happened with the first digital audio player. Kane Kramer, currently chairman of the British Inventors Society, filed a patent in 1981 for the world's first digital audio player (a device which looked almost exactly the same as today's iPod). Technology at the time was not what it is today. Kane would present his prototype and people would question where all the moving parts were. The market could not understand the concept of no tape: 'What is the music recorded on?' they would ask. The problem was that he was just too futuristic for the market and it wasn't until 20 years later that digital music and digital music players were embraced by a wider society. Apple continue to make millions from the iPod. Kane Kramer was simply ahead of his time.

Understanding in detail the answers to the above five questions will not only ensure that you get the timing of your launch right but also that you are extremely in tune with your customers' needs and desires and therefore best equipped to become an outstanding contributor to a highly competitive market.

Judge the value of your ideas critically.

Making a balanced decision

Being your own judge is not nearly as easy as it sounds but it is an essential skill. Constantly showering yourself with praise is not going to help you address the harsh realities of your situation constructively. Criticising and undervaluing all of your actions will do very little for your motivation, confidence and self-esteem. This type of mentality will also hinder your

❝ you need to be positive to take action and to maintain a healthy mindset to make balanced decisions ❞

progress. You need to be positive to take action and to maintain a healthy and balanced mindset to make balanced decisions.

Six Thinking Hats

I went through a stage of disciplining myself to the Edward De Bono Six Thinking Hats theory. I would consciously try to view a subject or a situation from each of the different perspectives and to draw a balanced conclusion as a result. Now this has become inherent in my mindset. I don't make decisions as rapidly but I tend not to change them as often either.

Edward De Bono offers you six different coloured hats which you wear to adopt a different mindset. For a specific period of time, you allow yourself to only wear one hat and to only think thoughts aligned with the mindset it represents. By wearing each hat for the same length of time, you consider your subject from every angle. Adopting either a positive, negative, creative, intuitive or purely factual approach helps you begin to really understand what you are thinking about. Over time this helps to give you a rounded viewpoint and assists you in making the right decision.

Look up the De Bono Six Thinking Hats principles if you are interested in learning more about this approach. Dr De Bono has his own website and copies of his Six Thinking Hats book are readily available through most book shops.

The Whether? Forecast™

I have adopted the De Bono principles and altered them slightly to suit my own needs. *The Whether? Forecast*™ is rather easier to remember and is my tool to create a balanced mindset. Use *The Whether? Forecast*™ method to decide whether to do this or whether to do that. It can be a very constructive way to make a balanced decision or you can apply it to add depth to your brainstorming sessions.

Try it out a few times. The more you practise, the more it will become second nature to view a problem constructively from all angles.

1. Identify your subject, conundrum or area of thought clearly.
2. Consider how much time you want to spend thinking about it.

3. Divide this time into 10 even portions.

4. Discipline yourself to spend each allocated portion of time to thinking only in one particular mindset. In other words, if your brainstorming session is 1 hour long, spend 6 minutes considering the lie of the land; 6 minutes adding in all external influences in the form of winds; 6 minutes thinking only 'sunshine' thoughts; 6 minutes thinking only rainy day, negative thoughts; 6 minutes considering your situation from a blue sky perspective and 6 minutes imagining it covered in snow. Having done this, spend a further 6 minutes reconsidering the lie of the land; 6 more minutes in 'sunshine mode' now that you have revisited your current position and 6 minutes considering the same scenario in 'rainy day mode'. Spend the last 6 minutes writing up *The Whether? Report*™ whereby you extract all of the relevant details that have emerged from your brainstorming session and present these as a summarised report.

Only now are you able to make a balanced decision and decide upon a clear course of action going forward.

As this way of thinking becomes familiar to you, you can add different factors to the basic modules if you like. Hail, tornado – you name it, you go for it! Modify this method to best suit you.

While you're at it, I should like to ask you to consider something else. Being an entrepreneur has its downsides as well as those moments of pure elation. In order to become a really amazing business owner, you are going to have to become a 'master of self'. In other words, you are going to need to know yourself inside out. You will need to know how to make the right decisions quickly and to have extremely good control over your emotions. You need to be honest with yourself. Are you really prepared to overcome all the challenges and objections that you are likely to face on this journey? Doing so requires you to understand how your emotions work.

❝ to become a really amazing business owner you are going to need to know yourself inside out ❞

Emotions are like the weather. How we predict what we are going to feel in any given situation is not necessarily how we end up feeling when we are there.

■ I know I am going to be happy and relaxed if I spend a day on the beach with friends.

The WHETHER? FORECAST™

Lie of the land	Your emotional gut reaction to your current situation. How does it feel, taste, smell, sound to you? The facts and figures exactly as they stand. Clearly and concisely presented without judgement, prejudice or preconception. Accept and understand your situation based on knowledge and proof.
Winds	All external influences that affect your decision-making process. These could be political, economical, technological or social. They might include strong emotions or other people's points of view. Winds blow towards and against you either as a gentle breeze or a strong gale. You can never capture or control the wind; you can merely harness it to your advantage.
Sun	The sun evokes positivity and optimism. Consider all of the benefits and advantages. The sun's bright light and the clear sky help you see into the distance. Consider the bigger picture and all that could be possible. In this mindset, you should be confident and light-hearted, happy, radiant and full of energy. Adopt a 'can-do' attitude.
Rain	The rain blocks drains and brings problems to the surface. Rainy days tend to be dark, damp and miserable. Approach this mindset as if you were living under a permanent dark cloud and with eternal pessimism. Consider all of the problems and disadvantages. Think of what you could lose. Adopt a 'can't-do' attitude and take extra precautions.
Blue sky	Surf the wide-open sky and think creatively. Explore boundless opportunities and freewheel over uncharted terrain. Be open to new ideas, however obscured the reality. Do not block, constrain or confine your thoughts to the known, but allow your mind to dance in limitless fantasy. Imagine you were floating above your situation and changes could be made as easily as moving chess pieces. What would you do?
Snow	Situations change quickly when it's snowing. It becomes harder to see the details and impossible to navigate. Heavy snow makes the world grind to a halt. This is your time to stop and take stock of your situation. Use your intuition. What is your gut reaction to your situation? Snow also covers up the details but brings to life a strong survival instinct in a harsher climate. Consider your situation as if it were covered in snow.
Whether? Report™	Conclude your creative-thinking session by delivering *The Whether? Report™*. Consider what has been important throughout the process, what new ideas have risen to the surface and what problems need immediately solving in order for you to progress. Deliver *The Whether? Report™* as an unbiased summary of your thinking and as a prioritised action list clearly stating your purpose.

- I know I am going to be sad if I go to a funeral.
- What we can't predict is the factors outside of our control.
- I can't predict sharing a joke and laughing at a funeral.
- I can't anticipate a pesky dog relieving itself on my picnic at the beach.

These are the unexpected events that make up reality. Learning how to enjoy and welcome these moments when our emotions are knocked off-balance by factors outside of our control instead of reacting to that loss of control with expressions of panic, anger and frustration is what distinguishes successful people from those who continually struggle. Apply *The Whether? Forecast*™ method of thinking as a quick mental exercise when you feel you are losing control and use this as a way of balancing out your emotions as well as making effective business decisions.

Remember, this is ultimately about your journey to success, what you are going to get out of it and what it is really worth to you and your family. Don't lose sight of what success means to you and those around you. Focus on reaching small milestones, one step at a time. Above all, value your freedom, your health and the fun times that motivate you, then consider the ultimate value of your idea in its true life-changing context. Think about it, value it and decide what you want to do next.

signposts to success

- If you are still unsure about the value of your idea and need to test it further by developing prototypes or evolving the original concept – turn to page 26.
- If you are absolutely convinced that you have got an original and winning idea then you need to be sure that you have claimed ownership of it – turn to page 36.
- If you think that you should plan your business better first – turn to page 55.
- If you decide that your best option is to bring your product to market by going in to production – turn to page 92.
- If you need further funding in order to make progress – turn to page 70.

3

How to develop your brainwave further

Stages of design development

So, having scribbled your idea down on the back of an envelope (or, better still, in a notebook) how do you turn it into something tangible and highly marketable? Well, there are two things that you need to be aware of:

- Firstly, you can't tell anyone about your idea if you are considering filing for intellectual property as doing so could seriously jeopardise your chances of protecting it and claiming official ownership over your creation.

- Secondly, you cannot possibly develop your ideas to perfection in isolation. You cannot design in a vacuum without taking the greater world – the people who will benefit or use your design and others like them – into consideration.

So, we find ourselves in a chicken and egg scenario. Do you:

(a) File for intellectual property prematurely so that you are better able to develop your invention with the assistance of others?

(b) Work on your invention independently by doing as much research into the needs and desires of others without actually exposing the details of your concept?

(c) Do both simultaneously?

The answer is, you do as much as you can without disclosing your ideas whilst keeping detailed chronological records of your development which could later be used to prove you as the originator of your idea.

If you are considering the possibility of securing intellectual property over your ideas then it is worthwhile knowing a little bit more about your rights before you start developing your ideas. Make sure you tell nobody about them unless you do so under the confines of a confidentiality or non-disclosure agreement. Read the chapter on intellectual property first (Chapter 4).

Seven stages of successful design development

1. Have a clear purpose
2. Explore the full potential
3. Examine what is possible
4. Re-assess and refine
5. Simplify the solution
6. Personify your products
7. Solidify the concept.

For now, let's concentrate on developing your idea. Development happens in stages and in cycles: seven different stages, to be precise, and an ongoing cycle of testing and perfecting. You begin by clearly setting out your purpose and intentions and then you brainstorm and explore the full potential of your fresh ideas. This will lead you to the point where you need to know more about what works and what doesn't. Are your ideas feasible? You will need to test them to find out. These tests, in turn, will lead to more ideas and a clearer understanding of your proposed solution. As your development continues, look for the simplest solutions to the problems that present themselves. As you simplify your ideas, so you will begin to add character and style to your design and finally, when you are satisfied with your end solution, you can solidify your concept as a marketable product.

❝ nothing happens instantly, nothing happens overnight and nothing is ever right the first time ❞

Nothing happens instantly, nothing happens overnight and nothing is ever right the first time. The sooner you accept this, the faster your progress will be. **Remember:** keep looking for problems from which to generate solutions and don't strive for perfection first time.

Design brief

A design brief is a written explanation outlining the aims, objectives and milestones of a design project.

An articulate brief is essential to the design process and will aid communication between the designers and the project drivers.

In essence a design brief will help you clearly communicate your intentions to anyone else involved in the development of your idea.

The design brief

Start by setting a strong design brief. Even though you can always come back and refine this brief and your development exposes alternative opportunities, it is important that you begin your development with a clear understanding of your intentions.

Once you have set yourself a concise design brief, you can begin to explore the real potential in the solution that you are proposing. This is a technique used by many successful designers and evident in the development of many iconic products. The Apple team, in particular, uses this technique to develop new designs.

Make a huge list of absolutely all of the features and benefits that your solution could offer in an ideal world. Don't be confined at this stage by how this will be achieved; just start with a giant wish list. Brainstorm, draw a mind map, and consider all of the information that you have gathered during your research. Sketch out or list on paper the absolute epitome of your perfect product, service or solution. This is what you are ultimately aiming for.

To start with, use a pen and paper to draw and sketch out your ideas. Make mistakes quickly and cheaply on paper where they are easy to correct. Later on, you can use computer-aided design packages or 3-D modelling software to create more accurate representations of your designs, but, for now, just concentrate on clarifying and focusing your own thoughts as you delve deeper and deeper into the details of your design.

Break the process down into manageable and measurable tasks so that you can start to attempt to prove the theory behind your concept. Do not be afraid of failure. It is through failing that you will learn best.

❝ do not be afraid of failure. It is through failing that you will learn best ❞

Do not be too concerned with what it looks like at this stage either; this will follow later. Concentrate instead on making each individual part of the process work and as feature-packed as possible. Get the 'cog and wheel' turning, so to speak. You are going to need to convince other people that this concept is ingenious so you had better be completely convinced that it works!

In order to prove that something works efficiently it is important that you test and optimise your theory. Measure and improve your results. Doing so can be difficult when you are obliged by the nature of confidential ideas to keep them secret. You are going to get the most accurate results from testing within a wide proportional representation of your target market but at this stage you may be advised to avoid disclosing your full ideas. It can be a delicate situation to handle.

I was convinced that bending the handle of the saucepan to form an ergonomic grip was the answer to making cooking safer and easier for everyone. In order to prove this theory, I needed to test people's grip strength. I didn't tell them what my research was related to but simply suggested that I was doing an ergonomic analysis of grip strength. I presented a series of weighted shapes (positioned at the height of a cooker though nobody knew this at the time) and looking nothing like saucepans, each with a different handle. In this way, I was able to measure, in a controlled environment and without any need to disclose my ideas, the benefits of my theory. It worked, and the results were conclusive.

Build prototypes and test your theory

Prototypes are going to be an essential part of your development and another area where you should keep both photographic and physical records. Prototypes can be made out of anything and everything. They can be as inexpensive or as costly as you need them to be in order to provide you with the results you are after.

They say that a picture speaks a thousand words; in this case, a prototype is worth a thousand pictures. By building a prototype, you will have something physical that you can hold and feel. You are much more likely to spot potential problems and hidden advantages in a prototype than you are in a 2-D drawing, so use your prototypes to find problems.

> **❝ they say that a picture speaks a thousand words; a prototype is worth a thousand pictures ❞**

Work on a cost-effective and manageable scale. If your plans are big and bulky then scale them down. Develop individual aspects as small and manageable components by examining the details before you attempt to bring the whole concept together.

James Dyson, when developing his revolutionary dual cyclone vacuum cleaner, built 5,127 failed prototypes before he finally got the technology behind his dual cyclone suction process working effectively. Much of Dyson's development focused on the technology behind the dual cyclone, so most of the prototypes he developed were in fact dual cyclones made out of old cereal packets, washing-up liquid bottles and anything else that came to hand. He continued this testing, evaluating and redesigning process through 5,127 cycles until finally he had reached a point where he was satisfied.

As his results became more specific and the need for accuracy more important, the standard and the quality of each prototype improved to include the testing and analysis of production-quality prototypes until finally the design was ready to go into the shops. Even now, almost 20 years on, the design of Dyson vacuum cleaners is constantly evolving.

James Dyson may have been methodical in the development of his idea and determined, against the odds, to prove his theory but he is not alone in his mindset. Make and test as many prototypes as is necessary to prove your theory.

Here is a list of good materials for making quick prototypes which you can use to develop your innovation:

- paper
- card
- clay
- modelling foam
- Polymorph™ – plastic granules that melt at boiling point and solidify to form a plastic object. The stuff is really easy to use and a very effective prototyping material. It is available in the UK from Maplins.
- MDF and plywood
- 3-D modelling software and computer-aided design.

Junk yards, skips and car-boot sales can also be great places to find components cheaply. Use your imagination – there are plenty of ways to create prototypes cost-effectively.

Start by taking action and let your results guide your next move. The problem many of us creative types have is that we just don't know when to stop developing. Our concept is seemingly never perfect. There is always more that can be done to improve a result or process and because of this, we forget when to stop. The development process becomes costly and there is seemingly no end to our relentless struggle to commercialise our ideas in the open market.

Stop looking for perfection. Allow your target market and profit margins to dictate what really works. Perfection will only come from evolving your ideas to best suit your customers' needs. Until you have the opportunity to really understand your customers' needs and test the effectiveness of your solution in the open market, you are never going to be able to measure accurately how perfect your idea really is. So, don't strive for perfection, strive to get something going instead.

> 66 don't strive for perfection, strive to get something going instead 99

Don't expect your audience to have your vision. Other people are unlikely to understand how you anticipate your idea will look and function unless they can see this clearly for themselves. Production-quality prototypes will help you convey your message more clearly. These are prototypes that look, feel and function exactly like the real thing. Having a production prototype produced is not always that cheap an exercise but it is a lot less expensive than opening up production for a product or service that fails to meet your customers' needs. It is much better to test the market with realistic-looking prototypes first.

You will find professional prototypers local to you, people skilled at making one-off pieces. These people are often able to make cost-effectively a single sample of your concept, based on the designs that you provide. Most universities, especially the ones with product design labs, also often offer prototyping services. Above all, the plant where you intend to have your products produced should be able to present you with a pre-production prototype before you commit to a volume order.

One of the most important reasons to have a pre-production prototype produced is so that you can check how accurately your design files are conveying the design you wish to produce. In order to benefit from any of the advanced prototyping techniques listed below you will need to have prepared accurate and detailed design files which, in this day and age, should be produced with the help of computer-aided design (CAD).

CAD programs often rely on specialist users trained in their functionality. I am not denying that you have the ability to teach yourself how to use the latest software and the capability to develop your own CAD files – this is what I did, after all – but I should warn you that I was trained as an industrial designer. You might prefer to enlist the help of a qualified designer at this stage. Most prototyping facilities have designers who are affiliated to them and consequently they are able to recommend who to work with. Elance.com is a great platform for finding people with these skills very effectively, LinkedIn and other such professional networks will also point you towards the right individual, as will design colleges, which tend to offer a plethora of affordable candidates. Just remember ... when you pay peanuts you attract monkeys!

Ask yourself what type of skills and areas of expertise the right designer would need to have. Be specific about what you expect them to do and how long you expect it to take. Be wary of sweeping statements or giving the designer too much free rein. What you lack in confidence, you make up for in vision. No designer will share the same vision as you. Be assertive when you describe it as only this way will you get what you actually want.

Advanced prototyping techniques include:

- **Rapid prototyping** This involves producing complex and accurate shapes quickly and as one-off pieces using computer-aided design to effectively print three dimensionally. Data is read from a file and an additive manufacturing machine is then used to lay down successive layers of liquid, powder or thin sheet material to build up the model through a series of predefined cross sections.

- **Laminated object manufacturing** This works in a similar way to rapid prototyping by laying down layers of a material (usually paper) to build a complex shape or form.

- **SLA modelling** Stereo lithography models are generated from 3-D CAD data by locally curing a resin using an ultra violet laser. Each section through the model is plotted in typically 0.1mm layers. A removable lattice is generated to support areas of the model that would otherwise deform. This is an ideal way of producing a complex component or a mould for vacuum or RIM casting (see below)

▪ **Fused deposition modelling (FDM)** This is a technique that generates models by extruding a controlled bead of molten polymer through a fine nozzle. Each section through the model is plotted at typically 0.15mm intervals. A support structure is simultaneously formed which is removed by hand after the model is completed. Although models show a slight stepping effect, they are dimensionally accurate, stable when exposed to light or water, and can be easily hand finished to produce a smooth, paintable surface. Models may be built from ABS or polycarbonate materials.

▪ **Vacuum casting** This is a simple way of generating one or more polyurethane components and can be a highly efficient way of producing more than one part that looks exactly the same. A sheet of polyurethane is heated and then lowered over a pre-formed mould (usually created using SLA or FDM techniques) and then drawn around the mould under vacuum until it cools to form the same shape. The mould can then be removed and reused multiple times.

▪ **Reaction injection moulding (RIM)** is a short- to medium-run production process using polyurethane resins. The temperatures and pressure within the mould cavity are lower than with conventional injection moulding and therefore larger pieces or small-run productions can be produced relatively cost-effectively.

This whole process of creating prototypes and testing your designs aids you to refine and simplify your solution. Ultimately, you are aiming to provide valuable features and benefits that are intuitive to use yet remain hidden within a simple solution to the problem you identified in your brief. The more you refine your development, the more you will begin to simplify these features and accommodate them within your solution as easy to explain and instinctive to use and benefit from.

66 **you need to give your ideas a personality of their own; by doing so, you will also be setting your brand values** 99

Next, you should be concentrating on personifying your design. Personifying a product or service is all about giving it character – that 'Ahh factor', if you will – something that endears your offerings to your customers, something people can fall in love with and cherish as something that appeals to their sense of humour or complements their prestige. In short, you need to give your ideas a personality of their own and, by doing so, you will also be setting your brand values.

Consider what it is that really matters about your product. Why is this important and who really cares? Once you have identified these values, you can begin to list the core characteristics that you would like to portray through your concept. Use this information to integrate such attributes into your designs.

Style is often associated with black and chrome; red can reflect passion, love or even anger; green and blue produce calm, tranquil connotations. Green can also mean 'Go!'. Consider the aesthetics of your product and what semantic message you want these to convey through the use of colour, shape, form and feel. Use this to further complement your design.

Take it back to the drawing board again. Now that you have worked out what components are essential to its function, you can begin to consider the limitations within which it must also look beautiful or display its character. Work with clay and card and other prototyping materials to develop the aesthetic appearance of your idea and then start to bring the two aspects of form and function together.

Neither form nor function should ever be addressed in isolation. This is why you will find the design process takes you round and round in circles from your sketch pad to the prototypers and back again until you eventually reach a satisfactory conclusion. Only then can you start to solidify the concept.

Up until this point your designs have remained fluid, reliant on their function and form as much as on that of the other components around them. Work with the parts that have been finalised first and use the aspects that remain fluid to link the whole together. Continually consider how best you can simplify each process.

One of my design teachers always used to talk about elegant simplicity being an asset to all good design and I still stand by this principle. It is always best to start with a long list of as many potential features and benefits as possible – the ultimate wish list, if you will. From this you can begin to break each feature and benefit down into its simplest form, decide what is essential and what would add value and remove what is unnecessary or overcomplicated. You are effectively trying to concentrate all of your ideas down into a simplified overall solution. Be prepared for hidden eventualities. Sometimes, no matter how much you develop something, you cannot foresee what might go wrong. It is for this reason that the process of developing your ideas is never really over.

When I first imported one container of cookware from the Far East, the design of my ergonomic handle featured a black and grey silicone marking that indicated the best hand position for the user's grip. It looked great and the black thumb grip clearly indicated where the thumb should go. But, it didn't work. People didn't really understand that this was where their thumb should go and I didn't realise that this black thumb grip was going to cause such a problem.

In fact, it was a manufacturing nightmare. Ladies in the factory were developing a repetitive strain injury fitting the thumb grip to the handle of a design that had actually been developed to prevent such an injury. By the time the saucepan reached somebody's kitchen, the thumb grip would last about six weeks before deciding it was time to fall out. It was expensive in production, causing unhappy customers and not really doing its job. It was time to go back to the drawing board ... and so the design evolved.

Developing and optimising an idea is an unending and rewarding journey. Do not expect instant perfection and make progress by measuring your results.

signposts to success

- If you decide that you need to secure your official intellectual property rights – turn to page 36.
- If you think that it is advisable to plan your business before proceeding – turn to page 55.
- If you're now ready to tell the world about your amazing idea by disclosing it publicly – turn to page 47.

4

How to secure your intellectual property

What is intellectual property?

'Intellectual property' (IP) is a term applied to creations of the mind: your ideas and creations, whether artistic or commercial. Intellectual property rights grant you exclusive right to your intangible assets and, as with any legal rights, they are governed by a strict and defining law.

ff IP is a term applied to creations of the mind: your ideas and creations, whether artistic or commercial ""

For this reason you may wish to consult a qualified lawyer or specialist IP attorney who can assist you to best secure your rights. This chapter is by no means comprehensive. It is intended to give you a basic grounding in the subject of intellectual property so that you can make the most of the time you spend with professional people trained in this highly complex subject by getting further into the details.

So, to give you an overview:

Common types of intellectual property rights include copyrights, trade marks, patents, industrial design rights and trade secrets. Securing your rights will give you, as the creator of original works, the economic incentive to develop and share ideas through a form of temporary monopoly in the market.

Trade secrets

When you first come up with an innovative idea, you will effectively be holding onto a trade secret. Trade secrets, also known as **confidential** or **classified information**, are formulas, practices, processes, designs, instruments or a compilation of information which is not generally known or not currently in the public arena. A trade secret is often something by which a particular business or individual can obtain an economic advantage over competitors or customers.

If you wish to reveal a trade secret which has not been officially protected by intellectual property laws then you should only do so using a confidential disclosure agreement. A confidential disclosure agreement (or non-disclosure agreement or simply a confidentiality agreement) is an agreement between you and the party that you wish to disclose your idea to. The agreement protects you and prevents the other party from further exposing your idea or claiming the idea as his or her own. It is essential that you use such an agreement if you wish to secure your IP rights at a later date.

There is no set formula for a confidential disclosure agreement. Many standard confidentiality agreements are available online and most legal professionals should be able to advise on the best structure for such an agreement. The most important thing to ensure is that disclosing your idea does not in any way assign or share its ownership or entitle the person signing the agreement to discuss or reveal your trade secrets with anyone else. Overleaf is a standard confidential disclosure agreement that has been taken from the official UK Intellectual Property Office website. You will need to amend it to best suit your needs. **Remember:** If your agreement is too complicated it may become difficult to persuade people to sign.

" the more you tell people about your idea, the more you are jeopardising your chances of making it a success "

Be sure to keep good records of anyone who has signed your agreement and to whom you have revealed your idea. Don't forget, the more you tell people about your idea, the more you are jeopardising your chances of making it a success.

Until such time as you have secured your official intellectual property rights, it is imperative that you keep your idea and all records of your idea secret (these are your trade secrets). If your idea finds its way into the public domain – for instance, if somebody you have told about it mentions it in a blog or if a photograph or picture of your concept falls into the wrong hands – then it can be deemed to have been public knowledge and therefore is no longer patentable. As soon as you have filed for official ownership, you are free to start discussing your ideas,

Confidential Disclosure Agreement

Between: [Company name and address] and [Your name and address]

1. On the understanding that both parties are interested in meeting to consider possible collaboration in developments arising from [your name]'s intellectual property it is agreed that all information, whether oral, written or otherwise, that is supplied in the course or as a result of so meeting shall be treated as confidential by the receiving party.

2. The receiving party undertakes not to use the information for any purpose, other than for the purpose of considering the said collaboration, without obtaining the written agreement of the disclosing party.

3. This Agreement applies to both technical and commercial information communicated by either party.

4. This Agreement does not apply to any information in the public domain or which the receiving party can show was either already lawfully in their possession prior to its disclosure by the other party or acquired without the involvement, either directly or indirectly, of the disclosing party.

5. Either party to this Agreement shall on request from the other return any documents or items connected with the disclosure and shall not retain any unauthorised copies or likenesses.

6. This Agreement, or the supply of information referred to in paragraph 1, does not create any licence, title or interest in respect of any intellectual property rights of the disclosing party.

7. After X [numerals] years from the date hereof each party shall be relieved of all obligations under this Agreement.

Signed [Your signature]
For [Company name]
Date

Signed [Company representative's signature]
For [Company name]
Date

though I advise that you don't make too much of a song and dance about it until you have a product or service that you are ready to sell. Never underestimate how clever your competition can be. Despite all the patents and design registrations in the world, a cheeky competitor will always try to find a way around your protection. When you tell the marketplace about your ideas, make sure that you are ready to offer them the finished solution. Until then, keep quiet and remain unequivocally protective.

For most people, securing intellectual property rights means spending a small fortune with a government office to secure the privilege of producing their own idea. However, there are a few things that you can do to secure some of your rights for free.

Copyright

Copyright is an automatic right which applies to an original or piece of work that has been written down or recorded in some way. You do not need to apply for international copyrights, these are automatically granted at the point the original work has been fixed. This gives you, as the creator of the original work, exclusive rights to that work including its publication, distribution and adaptation for a certain period of time which can be anything from 25 to 125 years, depending on the nature of the work you are protecting.

It is definitely worth being aware of your copyrights and taking precise action to ensure that you have secured these. Above all, securing copyrights need not distract from your ongoing development and does not need to cost you a penny. All you have to do is keep records and mark these as being subject to copyrights.

Use the copyright symbol © followed by your name or the name of your company. (As a lone creator, I highly recommend that you use your own name even if you are operating under a company name – should external shareholders come into your business, or should your company not survive long term, the rights will remain in your name. You can always agree to assign these rights to your company in the future.) After your name, the copyright line should include the date and place of creation and the sentence 'All rights reserved.' For example:

© **Joe Bloggs, 6 May 2009, Kings Arms Pub, London UK.**
All rights reserved.

Copyright can protect the following:

- **original works** – works must be original to have copyright protection
- **literary works**, including novels, instruction manuals, song lyrics, newspaper articles, websites, software programs and some types of database

- dramatic works, including dance or mime
- musical works
- artistic works, including paintings, engravings, photographs, sculptures, collages, architecture, technical drawings, diagrams, maps and logos
- layouts or typographical arrangements used to publish a work – for instance, a book
- recordings of a work, including sound and film
- broadcasts of a work.

❝ by writing down or recording your idea, you are automatically fixing your copyright ❞

Copyright does not protect ideas, but it does apply to any medium. By writing down or recording your idea, you are automatically fixing your copyright. Copyrights do not replace patents, design registrations or trade marks but they do boost their validity.

The best thing about copyright is that it has been internationally standardised. Unlike any other form of official, registered intellectual property right, copyright is effective both within and outside the territory of creation. This means that if, for example, you have copyrighted a photograph and someone in another country creates a painting from this, you may be entitled to stop them from recreating your image or to demand a royalty or fee for the rights to do so.

So, given that as you neither have to apply for them nor pay for the privilege, securing your copyrights is definitely in your interest. This is why it really is imperative that you begin thinking with a pen and paper to hand. Your very first scribble on the back of a beer mat could secure you your rights in the future. Always keep records of your thought process and always remember to date these records as you go along.

If you have any early development drawings, notes or prototypes then keep hold of them. Backs of envelopes are good as the date on the stamp will give you an indication of when you had this brainwave, but try if you can to become more organised with your development thoughts. I find an A4 drawing book works. Remember to date each entry and to sign the front page. It is also a really good idea to include an 'If found, please return to ...' message.

Naturally, any electronic documents will also support your case. Remember to keep chronological records of the development of your idea, irrespective of what technology you use.

Post yourself proof to further protect your ideas

To provide further proof of the date of origination, write your idea down, including supporting drawings and specific details, add the copyright symbol, date and sign the page. Seal this in an envelope. Address it to yourself and sign across the envelope seal. Send it by registered or recorded delivery and, when you get it back, without opening the envelope, write a note on it to remind yourself of the idea that it contains. Store this envelope securely and never open it. Presenting this sealed envelope to any judge will add certified proof to your claim. When it comes to deciding who was indeed the original creator or the first person to come up with a new idea, dates and timing are crucial. The better proof you have of being first, the stronger your case will be. It is imperative that you are aware of this throughout the development process.

Patents, industrial design rights and trademarks

Once you have finalised your concept you are ready to secure your official rights, claim ownership of your idea and become recognised as the original creator. There are three main forms of official intellectual property and, in some cases, you may be entitled to secure rights in all three different sectors. They each serve a specific purpose and it is important that you understand the difference.

Patents protect new inventions and cover how things work, what they do and how they do it. They may also protect how something is made and what it is made from. A patent gives the owner the right to prevent others from making, using, importing or selling the invention without permission. It is a set of exclusive rights granted by a state to an individual or company for a limited period of time in exchange for the disclosure of an invention.

Industrial design rights protect the visual design of objects that are not purely utilitarian and will include the creation of a shape, the configuration of a pattern or colour or combination of these in three-dimensional form. Essentially, industrial design rights protect the physical appearance of a design.

Trade marks are signs or logos which distinguish your goods and services from those of your competitors. You can use your trade mark as a marketing tool so that your customers will always recognise your products or services.

Search of prior art

Before you begin the process of filing a patent application, trade mark or a registered design it is essential to conduct a search of prior art and existing intellectual property. Prior art is basically anything (copyrights, patents, design registration, designs, theory, pictures, products, etc) that is already in the public domain. If any prior art exists that is similar to or the same as your concept, your idea will not be considered original and you will not be granted ownership. This is why you need to research all prior art surrounding your subject so that you can be certain of the originality of the aspects you are seeking to protect.

Visit the British Library in London and use their advanced patent search facilities; scan the internet; ask a patent attorney to search on your behalf. Do what needs to be done to find out as much as you can before you start completing your own application process and only seek protection for aspects of genuine originality.

Applications for official intellectual property rights

Applications for official intellectual property rights are filed with the intellectual property office responsible for the particular territory in which you intend to protect your idea. Currently, no single office grants you worldwide patent rights so you will need to file in each territory individually. Here in the UK all patents, designs and trade marks are filed through the Intellectual Property Office, either directly by the applicant or via legal representatives such as patent attorneys representing the creator either as a company or an individual. Most offices provide clear guidance to their specific application process and, in many cases, you are able to file an application by filling out an electronic form online. It is worth consulting a legal professional or contacting the relevant intellectual property office before you attempt to file a patent, design registration or trade mark for the first time as you want to be sure that you complete the process correctly and word your application to give you maximum available coverage of your idea or concept.

The process itself is relatively simple. You complete your application, send this along with the appropriate fees to the relevant office and wait for them to issue you with a filing number. At this point, you are able to declare that you have a patent or design pending. In other words, you have filed your application and you are waiting to hear the result.

All applications are then published whilst the intellectual property office assesses their originality and seeks to establish if there is any prior art preventing you from securing your claim of original creation. This can take 6–18 months, although in some cases you might be able to apply for a priority procedure which will speed up the process if you deem this to be necessary. Once the office has made their assessment they will contact you to inform you if your claim has been granted or not. In the event that you are not granted one form of IP you may wish to consider what alternative forms of protection are available to you.

Filing for a patent

❝ if you are entitled to a patent then you should opt for this protection first ❞

As a general rule of thumb, if you are entitled to a patent then you should opt for this protection first; you can always file subsequent design registrations to further substantiate your protection at a later date. In order to file for a patent your invention must:

- be **new** and not known anywhere in the world
- have an **inventive step** that is not obvious to someone with knowledge and experience in the subject or simply an adaptation or combination of existing technologies
- be capable of being **made** or **used** in some kind of industry or capable of having a technical effect.

In order to file for a patent your invention must *not* be:

- a scientific or mathematical discovery, theory or method
- a literary, dramatic, musical or artistic work
- a way of performing a mental act, playing a game or doing business
- the presentation of information, or some computer programs
- an animal or plant
- a method of medical treatment or diagnosis
- against public policy or morality.

If you have a patent granted, you must renew it every year after the fifth year for up to 20 years' protection. This protection will give you the right to prevent others from copying, manufacturing, selling and importing your invention without your permission. Owning a patent also allows you to:

- **sell** the invention and all the intellectual property (IP) rights

- **licence** the invention to someone else but retain all the IP rights

- discuss the invention with others in order to set up a business or **commercial enterprise** based around the invention.

Patents are enforced as a civil matter, as are trade marks and copyrights, whilst design registrations are subject to criminal sanctions. In other words, to enforce a patent, trade mark or copyright you will need to go through the court system, whereas you may well be able to send the fraud squad in to deal with an infringement of a design registration.

Design registration

In the event that your idea does not qualify for a patent, or if you decide to further substantiate your intellectual property rights, a design registration can be used to protect the look and appearance of your product. A registered design will also enable you to sell or license your IP rights. Under the Hague Agreement Concerning the International Deposit of Industrial Designs (a treaty administered by the World Intellectual Property Organization), a procedure for an international registration exists. As an applicant, you can file for a single international deposit with WIPO or with the national office in a country party to the treaty. The design will then be protected in as many member countries of the treaty as desired.

> ❝ a design registration can be used to protect the look and appearance of your product ❞

A registered design can be a valuable asset that allows you to stop others from creating designs which are too similar to yours. Although a design registration will protect the visual appearance of a product, it does not offer protection for how it works or what it is made from.

In order to register a design your idea must:

- be **new**

- have **individual character** (the appearance or overall impression is different from other known designs).

So, if your idea involves products or articles which are unique because they look different from anything else currently available, then it might be worth your while considering registering the design.

Registering a trade mark

Registering a trade mark may also be important to you. A trade mark is a sign – for instance, words, logos or a combination of both – which can be used to distinguish your products or services as appearing from a unique source. This will add to the value of your brand and identity. A trade mark is identified by the symbols ™ (not registered) or ® (registered). It must be distinctive and should differentiate you or your goods and services from other providers in a similar field.

A registered trade mark:

◼ may put people off using your trade mark without your permission

◼ allows you to take legal action against anyone who uses your trade mark without your permission

◼ allows Trading Standards Officers or police to bring criminal charges against counterfeiters if they use your trade mark

◼ is your property, which means you can sell it, or let other people have a licence that allows them to use it.

> **66 a trade mark can be a valuable marketing tool and one which you can protect 99**

A trade mark can be a valuable marketing tool and one which you can protect in the event of somebody else trying to copy you. If you have a registered trade mark you can put the ® symbol next to it to warn others against using it. However, using this symbol for a trade mark that is not registered is an offence. A registered trade mark must be renewed every 10 years to keep it in force.

You are **not** able to register a trade mark if it:

◼ describes your goods or services or any characteristics of them – for example, marks which show the quality, quantity, purpose, value or geographical origin of your goods or services

◼ has become customary in your line of trade

◼ is not distinctive

◼ is a three-dimensional shape, if the shape is typical of the goods you are interested in (or part of them), has a function or adds value to the goods

◼ is a specially protected emblem

◼ is offensive

■ is against the law – for example, promoting illegal drugs; or

■ is deceptive. There should be nothing in the mark which would lead the public to think that your goods and services have a quality which they do not.

In order to place yourself in the strongest possible position and able to make a commercial success of your intellectual property, you need to boost your protection as much as you can afford. Given the fact that you are effectively laying the foundations upon which your business will be built, it is highly recommended that you ask for professional advice, especially with regards to filing a patent. Most lawyers, legal advisors and patent attorneys offer a free initial consultation, take advantage of this and use it to find out as much information about how best to protect your ideas as you can.

Good luck! Filing for intellectual property rights signifies a very exciting time in the life of your young business.

signposts to success

- ■ If you think you need to better **plan your business** – turn to page 55.
- ■ If you have decided to go into **production** of your invention yourself – turn to page 92.
- ■ If you are ready to **launch your idea publicly** – turn to page 47.
- ■ If you need to **raise finance** before you can carry on – turn to page 70.
- ■ If you want to know more about **marketing** your IP – turn to page 112.
- ■ If you are interested in knowing what options you have, to make a **return on your IP investment** – turn to page 81.

5

Publicly disclosing your brainwaves

When to disclose

Having secured your intellectual property, you are finally in a position to be able to disclose your ideas publicly. The best time to do so is as soon as you are ready.

If you have not yet secured your intellectual property, you should not be considering revealing your trade secrets to anyone. Make sure you secure your intellectual property first. To find out more about how to do this turn to Chapter 4.

Your changing role

As soon as you have filed your official intellectual property rights and been given a filing date, you are at liberty to start promoting your business concept to the world. At this point, your role changes entirely. Up to this stage, you have been the judge and jury of your remarkable new ideas; you have been unable to ask too many people for their input and you have been forced to rely on your research and your good judgement.

If you have done your homework right, you will have fully convinced yourself that you have a truly remarkable idea and one with the potential to hold huge commercial value. **Now step aside and adopt a new role.** You are no longer the judge. You are no longer the jury. The decision about the greatness of your invention is now out of your hands. You should almost breathe a sigh of relief. That responsibility has gone. You have put it into the hands of a much more qualified group of people: your target market.

££ from the moment you disclose your idea publicly you must become an ambassador for it ££

But your job isn't complete. Your role has simply changed. From the moment you disclose your idea publicly you must become an ambassador for it. You are now in charge of **promotion** and **early market analysis**. This is also the time to draw as much public attention to what you are doing as possible. Not only will this help with the sales and marketing of your idea but it will also help you make claims over your original ownership. If you can appear, with a photo, in your local paper, what better proof is there of you being the original creator of your new idea?

Set a deadline

The important thing about public disclosure is not to delay the date when you do it. Set yourself a deadline and stick to it. This is important. As creative individuals, we tend to drift aimlessly. As entrepreneurs, we need to be clear and focused about what we are doing and putting a deadline in place can be a great way of achieving this. Time is money, so they say. The longer you leave it, the more money you stand to lose.

I encourage you to make your deadline a public one. Choose a show, exhibition, seminar or event, for example – something that impacts other people as well as yourself. Public deadlines are always easier to stick to! If you have committed to attend a show or exhibition, for example, then you *have* to get your work completed in time and this can really accelerate your progress.

Preparation

Before you disclose publicly, it is important that you are well prepared, especially if you intend meeting and discussing your innovation with other people. Effectively your job as the innovator or creator is complete – now step back and adopt an entrepreneur's mindset. Start planning your public disclosure properly and set a realistic deadline that you can really start to work towards. There is a lot to be done if you want to be taken seriously.

> 66 your job as the innovator is complete – now step back and adopt an entrepreneur's mindset 99

When I first publicly disclosed the Doctor Cook design, I did so at the British Invention Show. That was back in 2004. I remember being so nervous that I crashed the car in the car park outside Alexandra Palace, where the show was being held. I felt a fool. I walked into the vast hall and everyone's inventions, innovations and business concepts looked amazing.

Mine seemingly paled into insignificance and my hands trembled as I began to set up my stand.

My problem was, I lacked confidence. But I was incredibly well prepared. Had I realised how well prepared I was at the time, I would have put aside my jittering nerves but as it was, I doubted my own ability, I doubted the quality of my research and I doubted the benefits of my design. You have to learn to overcome this.

Success is failure turned inside out, the silver lining to the clouds of doubt. You need to seek out that silver lining; you need to get the butterflies in your tummy flying in formation; you need to appreciate that you are outside your comfort zone and allow this knowledge to console you. There are going to be people in that room in a much worse state than you are. **Now is your time to shine.**

Your aim and your audience

Before any public disclosure or presentation of your invention, innovation or new idea, you need to give a bit of thought to what you intend to get out of the event. How is publicly disclosing your idea going to benefit you and the growth of your business and how do you intend to achieve these results? What is your aim here?

> ❝ how is publicly disclosing your idea going to benefit you and the growth of your business? ❞

- Is it simply – but importantly – to **gain public recognition** for having been the inventor and further **confirm the ownership** of your intellectual property in the process? In which case, you will want to target the media, to enter industry awards and to receive the public accolade you deserve.

- Is it to **promote your new business** by attracting new customers and converting these into profitable sales? In this case, you need to be prepared to collect everyone's details as it is very unlikely that you will make an actual sale on your first point of contact. Come up with a way of collecting the contact details of every new potential customer you meet. You could run a competition, for instance, or give away a free report on the new technology you have developed, or simply ask for a business card, or invite each visitor to fill in a visitors' book so that you can subsequently use this contact information to build relationships with these people and convert them into valuable customers later on.

▓ Is it to **generate wider industry contacts** so as to expand your business through joint ventures and common goals? To do this successfully you will need to be clear about who you would like to meet. Are you looking for investors, manufacturing partners, distribution partners or business mentors? Think about this thoroughly and make a list. Doing so will help you be more focused about who you target and help you attract the right people to your stand.

Filling out a table like the one below is a good way of focusing your thoughts.

Market, message, media: the multi-step approach

TARGET AUDIENCE	MARKETING MESSAGE	MESSAGE DELIVERY
Who do you want to meet?	What do you want to tell them?	How will you communicate this message?

Think about who you want to meet or who your target audience is, then decide which message you need to deliver to them to capture and sustain their interest. Decide what media you are going to use to deliver it to them. Will you give them something to take home or follow your conversation up with a letter or email later? Are you simply going to talk to the people you meet at the event? How will you attract them to you when you are there? Are you planning on sending out a press release or posting notices online? Do you intend to contact individuals directly and invite them to visit you at your show or will you arrange an appointment at their offices? The clearer you are, the more successful you will be in your outcome.

❝ adopt a multi-market, multi-media, multi-message approach ❞

Remember: In the world of business, action creates momentum and momentum generates magnetic attraction. Adopt a multi-market, multi-media, multi-message approach and do all you can to generate a strong magnetic field around you and your ideas and to draw the right attention towards you.

The elevator pitch

Plan how you intend to present your business and brand. As well as the product or service, have you considered what characteristics or personality you want to convey through your promotional messages? If you are going to be selling your business concept to other people then you will need to develop your **elevator pitch**. This is a 3-minute summary (or rather, a quick presentation that, in theory, lasts no longer than an elevator ride) – a succinct presentation of your idea that grabs people's attention and invites them to find out more about how you can help them.

If you're confident that you have developed an award-winning elevator pitch, write it down in a box like the one overleaf. If not, spend some time brainstorming about what the most important messages are that you need to convey and in what order the person listening will find these most interesting.

If you were stuck in the lift with somebody you really wanted to meet, what would you tell them about your idea? A successful elevator pitch summarises the benefits of the idea; it portrays the unique selling points of the business clearly and concisely, and invites the listeners to ask to know more.

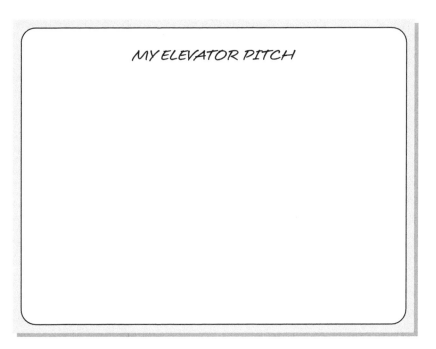

Remember to target this pitch at the people you are presenting to. Different people respond in different ways and it is important that you speak a language your target audience understands and is stimulated by. Consider the aspects of your concept that most interest the person you are talking to and tweak your elevator pitch accordingly.

Your elevator pitch is always a work in progress. The more times you practise it, the better you will become. You could always go and stand in an elevator in a busy building and practise till you've got your audience begging you to tell them more!

Having your elevator pitch ready and a clear idea of what you hope to achieve from the event will dramatically increase the chances of a successful outcome.

Presentation

Naturally, you will need to do your proposal justice and this is where presentation techniques become important.

❝ most people make a decision about whether to do business with you within the first 5 minutes of your meeting ❞

Most people make a decision about whether or not they want to do business with you within the first 5 minutes of your meeting – 60% of people will actually make this decision within the first 2 minutes and 80% will have confirmed their opinion within 5 minutes. However, it's not how quickly the decision is made that is important but the factors on which it hinges.

The first thing most people will subconsciously judge you on is your **attitude** and the second thing is your **appearance**. And, in the case of publicly disclosing your invention, we are talking about the attitude and appearance of your products and services too.

So, prepare for your presentation and be sure to show off your ideas at their best. Look and feel the part yourself and remember to enjoy and stay positive throughout the whole event. Even if people are critical of what you show them, take this as being constructive. Remember, this is the first time anyone other than you and your close friends and family have seen your idea and criticism is what you should be listening out for.

You know that your idea is good or you would never have pursued it this far. Praise and compliments will make you feel great but they are not necessarily going to help you develop your concept. Listen out for objections instead. When somebody raises an objection, embrace it and ask them to clarify it in detail. Understanding people's objections will help you overcome them. If you have done your research properly, you may even have the answer to their objection to hand and this can be a sure way to impress any of your new-found judges.

Listen and learn from everything you hear people say or see them do in response to your presentations. Ask lots of questions and gauge the answers and reactions. Keep your eyes open for new opportunities; stay focused towards the target audience you set out to meet; collect everyone's contact details and target your message to meet their needs.

Remember to pat yourself on the back too. Reaching the point of public disclosure is a real milestone. You have reduced the odds of your success considerably. Having started out with a 1 in 33,000 chance of making your idea a real success, you are now at the stage of 1 in 3. Remember, with the right kind of attitude, you could be on the fast track to reaping the rewards – or winning an international accolade.

signposts to success

- If you would like to know more about the British Invention Show, please visit www.thebis.org

- If you would like to know more about writing a press release, turn to page 112.

- If you are interested in understanding how to convert new-found contact details into profitable sales, turn to page 101.

- If you would like to know more about developing your brand and supporting marketing materials, turn to page 146.

- If you are concerned that you need a prototype, turn to page 26.

- If instead you are considering how to manufacture your invention, turn to page 92.

6

How to plan your business

The purpose of planning

As soon as you mention business planning, most people automatically think of a formal business plan. The very prospect of writing and preparing one of these seemingly lengthy documents petrifies most of us into avoiding the subject entirely. However, if we are put off by the prospect of planning, our businesses are going to suffer as a result.

Planning your business is an essential entrepreneurial pastime which is both fascinating and fun. I want you to become inspired by the very prospect of making plans for your future. Forget what you think you know about business planning and concentrate on what is really important when it comes to formalising your plan.

As we have already identified, turning your brainwave into a brilliant business is a journey. You start with an idea and gradually, as your adventure unfolds, you begin to blossom into an entrepreneur with real vision and your idea into a business with boundless opportunities. Sometimes this happens by accident but, as with most other successful journeys, you are much more likely to reach your intended destination if you actually plan where you want to go and how you intend to get there.

This is the purpose of developing a business plan. Planning helps you to understand clearly what your business does and how it has come about. It enables you to define your objectives; set a schedule for achieving these; monitor whether you are meeting your targets so that you can best allocate resources and manage your priorities. A business plan will help you identify areas of potential growth and hazards which may arise in the future. Having a strong business plan is essential to attract potential investors and a highly valuable tool with which you can inspire and motivate your team.

The purpose of business planning

- Define business purpose.
- Achieve business objectives.
- Meet business targets.
- Allocate resources.
- Manage priorities.
- Identify growth areas.
- Signpost problems.
- Attract funding and investment.
- Inspire and motivate the team.

Think of your business plan as an agenda if you like, specifying your direction and your anticipated performance. It needs to address the following questions:

- Where do you want to be?
- Where are you now?
- How are you going to get there?
- How is this going to be financed?

Apply your imagination, use your creative talents, be inspired by the prospect and use the time you spend planning your business to really inject some fresh energy and focus into what it is that you intend to achieve.

As your idea grows and develops, so will your business plan. It will evolve in cycles: annual cycles, biannual or even quarterly cycles, depending on how often you set aside the time to bring it up to date. The earlier you can start formalising your business plans, the easier you will find them to update and improve as your business grows and the better prepared you will be for the future.

Set aside the time to work *on* your business as opposed to the day-to-day routine of working *in* your business. Working *in* your business is what most people tend to do every day – servicing your customers' needs; development of new products or marketing material; managing staff and keeping accurate accounts – all of these activities are effectively what you do when you are working in your business. Working *on* your business, on the other hand, is the work you do planning your direction and managing your growth; the time you take to develop and work on the structure and future of your business. Make sure you dedicate time to working on your enterprise as well as in it and begin the process of formalising your plans today.

My intention is to inspire you to think about your future. For this reason we are first going to look at planning your business and then we will consider how to present this information as a formal business plan.

Personal motivation

Planning your business informally

Have you ever thought about plans for your future? At school and during formal education it is natural for us to consider where a specific decision might lead us. As we get older, seemingly we forget to retain this frame of mind. Our progress slows down and our goals become harder to reach as a result.

So, before you can even start to consider planning your business you need to be clear what your own personal objectives actually are. The last thing that you want to end up doing is planning a role for yourself within your business that you absolutely hate doing or force yourself, through your own inconsistent plans, to live a lifestyle you never intended.

❝ be clear about your own personal objectives and then start to formalise plans for your business ❞

Be clear about your own personal objectives and then start to formalise plans for your business.

Answer this question as honestly as you can: **What motivates you?**

According to Freud, all human behaviour is motivated by the desire to feel pleasure. That motivation is organised and directed by two instincts: aggression and sexuality. When broken down further (and after our basic needs for food, sleep and safety have been met) these equate to four simple, modern motivating factors: **hate, money, sex** and **love** – pretty much in that order. So, what are the driving forces compelling you to turn your brainwave into a business?

Your motivation is going to be what carries you through some of the tougher times that might lie ahead. You need to be very clear what it is that really motivates you and you need to make sure that your plans fuel you with enough of these factors to sustain further growth. **Remember:** You are the driving force behind your business. If you lack motivation then this will reflect in the performance of your business.

> ❝ if you lack motivation then this will reflect in the performance of your business ❞

Next, consider what this motivation is actually worth to you in monetary terms. Put a value on your ideal lifestyle and identify how much you need to be earning each year to achieve this way of living.

- How much does the car cost?
- How much does the house you love cost?
- How much will it cost to avoid having to do the things you hate, like cleaning and ironing?
- How many holidays do you need?
- What hobbies do you wish to pursue?

Consider all of this in an absolutely ideal environment and then identify what it will cost you to sustain. This will become your personal target. Next, consider your age. When do you want to be living this dream? In other words, how many years are you giving yourself before all of this has to become a reality?

These two factors need to be built into your business plan (plus or minus a tolerance level for what is real and what is actually achievable). Don't be ashamed to set your targets high. It is amazing what you can achieve when you truly resolve to.

Having given serious thought to your personal plans you can start to align these with plans for your business.

SWOT analysis

Start planning by understanding where you are starting from. The fastest and most effective way to survey your current position – the position you personally find yourself in as well as the position in which your company currently stands – is to run a SWOT analysis. SWOT stands for strengths, weaknesses, opportunities and threats. Split a large sheet of paper into four quarters and brainstorm. Be honest and open with yourself. Use the *Whether? Forecast*™ method to further your balanced thinking and take a realistic snapshot of your current situation.

Being a small start-up can be an opportunity: your business is flexible and you can move and change direction quickly. Being a small start-up can also be a threat: you are vulnerable to fierce competition and your ideas are not yet secure. It can be a weakness too, especially if you are running on low resources. Add each element to the relevant box. Knowing what tools you have to hand, what strengths and opportunities you can use to your advantage can help you strengthen your position. Being aware of the threats and weaknesses within your business can help you take defensive precautions or take action to strengthen your position as you move forward.

Setting goals

❝❝ break your ultimate aim down into manageable, measurable and achievable tasks and set these as your business goals ❞❞

Remember: This is all about your journey and NOT about an ultimate destination. Having understood your starting point it is imperative that you **set your mission**. What mission are you on? What do you ultimately hope to achieve? What are you campaigning to change? If you have done your research correctly then you will have answered these questions already. Be clear with your answers and summarise them as 3 strong sentences. Break your ultimate aim down into manageable, measurable and achievable tasks and set these as your business goals which will help grow your business.

Essentially there are only **3 real ways to grow a business**:

1. You can increase the amount of each customer transaction.
2. You can increase the frequency with which each customer transaction takes place.
3. You can increase the number of customers in your business.

However, before you can consider growing your business, you need to set about creating a business to grow. This means developing a product or service with which to trade and doing so is likely to require an investment

S.W.O.T. Analysis

Strengths	Weaknesses
Opportunities	Threats

of time, know-how and resources. Consider what skills, funds and further action are required to create a business that you can grow.

You need to turn your designs into marketable products, produce these products for resale and then market and sell this service before you see any return at all on your initial investment.

▨ How much will it cost to get you to this stage?

▨ How are you going to fund this development?

▨ Having overcome the above two hurdles how do you propose recovering and then profiting from this initial investment?

Break-even analysis

It is important to consider the financial implications of your business plan in depth if you want to minimise your own risks as well as those that may be undertaken by any investor or financier considering supporting your growth. Essentially, you need to weigh up the facts and the figures, for instance:

▨ What is the size of your potential market?

▨ What proportion of this market will you need to capture in order to sustain your business activities and control the growth of your company?

▨ Who are your competitors?

▨ How many of them are there and what potential threats do they pose to your business?

These sorts of questions all give rise to a further question: How much is it going to cost you to sustain your business? Every business has overheads: fixed operating costs that need to be met whether the business is generating a profit or not. Your overheads include the rent of your operating premises; the cost of your staff salaries; your salary; professional fees; electricity; rates; repairs; supplies that are essential to your ability to function and sustain your business. List these and be clear about what they total. This is how much you are going to need to turn over in order to break even.

Breakeven point = Fixed costs / (Unit selling price – Variable costs)

In business and economics the **break-even point** (BEP) is the point at which costs or expenses and revenue (the income you receive from your normal business activities) are equal. There is no net loss or net gain and you are said to have 'broken even'. Knowing the point at which your business will break even will help you measure and monitor the profits (or loss) that your business is generating. Your break-even point should be clearly specified in your business plan. It is also a great figure to have in your head. If you know that you need to make 100 sales a month in order to break even then you have a clear target upon which you can focus your activities.

In order to calculate your break-even point, you need to know at what price you intend to sell each unit and how much it is going to cost you to produce and deliver. The cost of creating and delivering each unit is what is known as the variable cost as it will vary depending on how many units you sell. The difference between the two is your gross profit.

Understanding the results of your break-even analysis is important in ascertaining the likelihood of you achieving the success you are aiming for. If selling the number of units required to break even is not feasible then you may need to reconsider your business model. Can you reduce your fixed or variable costs or can you increase the selling price of each unit? Be realistic about the goals you are setting yourself.

Average customer value

Having understood how many units you need to sell in order to break even, it is equally useful to understand what your average customer value is (or what you aim for it to become). If you are hoping to develop long and lasting relationships with your customers, you are also hoping that they are going to buy from you more than once. You need to know the average number of times a customer is likely to buy from you and the average length of time that they are likely to stay loyal to your business.

As a conservative rule of thumb, this figure is often calculated on the basis that your customers will stay loyal to you for three years. If each unit price is £10 and the average customer buys 10 units from you a year, over a three-year period, the average value of this customer is £300. Knowing this figure will help you clearly identify how much investment (in marketing and promoting your business) you can profitably make to gain and retain loyal customers.

(Total number of sales in one year ÷ Total number of customers in one year) × Average customer life-time loyalty in years = Average lifetime value of your customers

At the start of any business you are dealing with the unknown. As your business grows, as more customers buy from you, as you begin to know how much it will actually cost you to gain and retain a new customer, you will begin to build a series of results from which you can deduce more accurate averages and forecast your future more precisely. As with everything you do, your business plan will never be perfectly accurate first time. If you take the time to consider and plan your potential properly, if you use your plan as a dynamic model from which to reflect on your achievements and monitor your progress, and if you set aside constructive time to do just that, you will soon start to notice the benefits of such a disciplined approach.

Forecasting the financials

This is as much about how wrong you are as it is about how right you could be. In the early days, forecasting your figures feels a little bit like plucking numbers out of thin air. As you further your research and development, as your fixed and variable costs become clearer, and as early market response begins to offer you better indications of your business potential, your plan will start to become a more focused and accurate document upon which you can base your future. Take time to update it regularly.

For further help forecasting the financials in your business plan then please visit our website www.FromBrainwaveToBusiness.com where you can download an Excel template that will help you predict your sales forecasts, establish your profit or loss and monitor your cash flow.

You will need to include cash-flow models and profit and loss accounts in any formal plan you present, so again it is worth becoming familiar with these tools sooner rather than later.

Formalising your business plan

Formalising your business plan is all about presenting the information that you have collated above in a formal document that clearly and concisely lays out your growth strategy in a manner that anyone can understand. For this reason, it is important to adhere to the standard presentation format. Bankers, investors and financiers tend, in general, not to be as naturally creative as innovators and ideas people. You need to present a proposal that speaks to such individuals in language that they will understand. Despite you believing that your creative input adds value this is not necessarily the case when it comes to producing a formal business plan.

> **" consider who you are presenting your plan to and tailor the content and format to best suit their needs or expectations "**

Keep it simple. Use the list below as a guide to what you need to include. Use clear formal language. Use the third person instead of 'I' and be sure that the document looks clean and professional. Consider who you are presenting your plan to and tailor the content and format to best suit their needs or expectations.

Laying out the content of a formal plan

Business plan contents list

Executive summary
- (the opportunity)

Company overview
- Mission
- Goals and objectives
- Ethos and philosophy
- Market overview
- Industry overview
- Core strengths and opportunities
- Legal status
- Products and services
- Description
- Competitive advantages
- Pricing structure

Marketing plan
- Market overview – Trends and economics
- Niche opportunity
- Aligned features and benefits
- Analysis of competition

- Promotional strategy
- Channels of distribution
- Summary of sales forecasts

Operational plan

- Production
- Location
- Distribution
- Legal environment

Management and organisation

- Key management team
- Professional advisors

Start-up expenses and capitalisation

Financial plan

- Profit and loss projections
- Cash flow projections
- Opening balance sheet
- Break-even analysis
- Risk analysis

Appendix

- Brochures and literature
- Patents and designs
- Blueprints and plans
- Letters of intent and testimonials
- Copies of contracts
- Other supporting material

1. The executive summary

This is your elevator pitch – a short, punchy and captivating paragraph that summarises what it is you plan to do and how you intend to achieve this. In reality, this is the most important paragraph of the whole plan. You need to stimulate the reader's interests and create a compelling desire to know more about you and your business. Failure to capture their attention at this stage could mean that the rest of the plan goes unread, so take the time to word this short paragraph properly.

The opportunity If you are using your plan to raise capital, then explain clearly what opportunity you are offering a potential investor, or the terms under which you can realistically repay a loan.

2. Company overview

State clearly the mission that you and your company are on and list the targets and objectives you are setting yourself. Make these specific and quantifiable. In this section you also want to explain your company ethos, including the values behind your brand and why these are important.

Next, summarise the market and industry you are entering and the opportunity that you have identified within this sector. Explain how and why you are capable of capitalising on this opportunity. In other words, describe the core strengths of your business and how these can be leveraged to maximise your potential in this market.

Conclude this section by stating the legal status of your business. Are you a limited liability company, a limited liability partnership, a partnership, a social enterprise or a sole trader? When did you set up? Explain the ownership of your enterprise.

If you are unsure about which trading structure would best suit your needs then contact Business Link, HM Revenue and Customs and/or Companies House who will all be able to provide you with up-to-date information on what your best options may be. You can also discuss your options with an accountant, solicitor or experienced professional who may be able to offer further, current information.

3. Products and services

Describe the products and services you are offering. Keep this concise and compelling. You can support this description with further details and pictures in the appendix of the plan. Focus on selling the features and benefits of your idea and how these provide you with a strong competitive advantage. Describe your pricing structure and any plans you may have to grow your product range in the future.

4. Marketing plan

A marketing plan seeks to explain the opportunity that exists within a market sector and how you intend to promote your products in this area.

Answering these 7 questions with 7 sharp sentences will help you write your marketing plan:

1   What is the purpose of your marketing plan?
2   What benefits do you provide to your customers?
3   Who is your target audience?
4   Where is the niche within this market sector?
5   What marketing tools will you use to reach your audience?
6   What is the identity of your business?
7   How much will you invest in marketing?

For a list of marketing tools please visit our website at www.FromBrainwave ToBusiness.com where you can download this for free.

5. Operational plan

This section will include specific details about how you intend to carry out operations within your business. How do you intend to produce your products or services? Will you be using external suppliers and, if so, who are they and how reliable are they? Do you have more than one source of supply or a back-up plan if your suppliers let you down? Where will your premises be based? Is there a reason for or competitive advantage in your location choice? Under what terms will you establish your location – for instance, a lease or a mortgage?

Having identified how you intend to create a product or service, how will you fulfil your orders or distribute your services? How efficient will your operation be and how will this efficiency be determined? Consider how you can improve the efficiency of your operations as your activities and demand for your products or services grow.

You should also include details of the legal environment in which you are operating. Is there any legislation that affects your business? Do you need permits or approvals in order to operate? What are the health and safety regulations that concern your industry or profession? Detail any insurance cover you have or may need and also give the details of any intellectual property rights, patents, trade marks or designs you have obtained or applied for.

6. Management and organisation

Describe your key personnel and the skills and know-how your business needs in order to survive and thrive. If you have a large team then present the personnel structure of your business in a flow chart. Identify where you need further resources and how you intend to bring these into your business. What professional advisors are supporting your business? Provide details of your accountants, lawyers, business mentors, etc.

7. Start-up expenses

If this plan is for a new business, explain the financial implications of setting up and starting operations. How do you plan to cover these costs?

8. Financial plan

This section seeks to turn all of the above information into numbers. Banks, financiers and potential investors will pay particular attention to this section, so be sure to get it right. If in doubt, your accountant should be able to help you. Visit our website at www.FromBrainwaveToBusiness. com and download the financial planning tools that are available. The series of Excel spreadsheets will help you create your sales forecasts, cash flow and profit and loss predictions.

“ make sure that you are able to elaborate, explain and justify any figures that your forecasts show ”

A word of warning: If the purpose of the plan is to raise capital for your business then you can expect to be seriously quizzed on your numbers. Make sure that you are able to elaborate, explain and justify any figures that your forecasts show.

9. Appendix

Use this section to further substantiate the information included in your plan. Add pictures of your product. Provide supporting marketing and promotional material and include details of any intellectual property rights you hold or have applied for. If you have developed blueprints for your business then add them here. Also include any comments that you have from customers or potential customers, copies of existing contracts or leases, details of your market research, any magazine articles or press features you might have been in and material that will further support and enhance the message that you are delivering in your plan.

Your business plan should be presented as a formal typed document. Include essential pictures, diagrams and tables or charts which make the information clearer and easier to understand but do not try to overcomplicate the presentation of this document with elaborate graphic design or sales-style marketing slogans. Keep the information concise, easy to understand and focused on the end objective or purpose of the plan. As with everything, test it first. Give it to one or two people and listen carefully to their feedback. Use this information to improve and optimise your plan before presenting it to other people.

It is important that you realise that your plan may contain confidential information about your business. You are completely entitled to ask anyone to sign a confidentiality agreement before you present them with your plan if you deem this to be necessary.

Remember: Your business plan is a dynamic working document. As your business grows, your plan will evolve, so set time aside to work on your business and not just *in* it! The more you practise planning your business the better at it you will become. Doing so can be very inspiring and motivating, especially when you start monitoring the massive amounts of progress you have made.

> **❝ set time aside to work on your business and not just in it! ❞**

---

signposts to success

- If you need advice on setting up a business, registering a company or becoming a legally trading entity with which to exploit your intellectual property then I suggest you use Google. HM Revenue and Customs, Business Link and any good accountant will be able to advise you on your options.

- If you are writing a business plan for the purpose of raising money then all of the above requires your consideration. However, there are a number of formal presenting techniques that you should follow and a series of precise questions that you need to answer – turn to page 55.

- If you are thinking, 'Oh heck! How on earth can I start selling to customers? I haven't even got a product yet.' – turn to page 26.

- If you need to start generating more sales and want to brush up on your sales skills – turn to page 101.

- If you want to consider how to grow your brand and assets – turn to page 146.

How to raise funds for your business

Eliminating perceived risk

Growing any business or developing a new idea is going to require a certain amount of growth or start-up capital. Raising funds successfully depends entirely on your ability to eliminate the perceived risk associated with your new business venture.

Essentially, it all boils down to you again. If you are prepared to ask other people to invest in you and your business then it is imperative that you are prepared to invest in yourself. The people with the money are going to be judging you as much as they are evaluating your product and business proposal.

Prepare yourself

Identify the situation you are currently in and take action to minimise your own personal risks. What are you doing to sustain your day-to-day life? Are you in a position to exist on a basic bread-and-butter income or are you desperate for the cash?

Being in a situation where you are personally reliant on an investment to survive will vastly weaken your position of negotiation. Banks and lenders seem more than happy to throw money at you when you don't need it. When you turn up on their doorstep with your begging bowl ... watch how fast the shutters come slamming down. Try to stabilise your situation with a sustainable bread-and-butter income which remains unaffected by the performance of your new venture.

Next, consider what you are bringing to the negotiating table. You are investing your time, the resources that are available to you and your knowledge and know-how. Does your offering include anything else? Do you have market experience or existing relationships with potential customers and clients? All of these factors are highly valuable and should not be overlooked when you are preparing to raise business funding.

Be prepared for some tough questions

Don't try to pull the wool over anybody's eyes – least of all your own. Be honest and up-front. Raise the difficult issues before anyone else gets a chance to. Identify your weaknesses and what threatens you and your business and prepare answers to how you propose overcoming this. This is a much more proactive approach to your presentation. Never leave a skeleton in the closet – it's bound to emerge at the most inappropriate moment.

❝ raise the difficult issues before anyone else gets a chance to ❞

Prepare your business

Prepare your business for investment by acknowledging the potential risks and taking active steps to minimise these.

The risks are massive. The probability of your brainwave or business plan having a fundamental flaw is far greater than that of you or your idea becoming a widespread success. Your belief in your capability to deliver on your business plan is purely subjective and you have got to acknowledge this both personally and from the point of view of any potential investor.

As creators and originators we have a tendency to believe in the potential of our brainwaves so passionately that it becomes almost impossible to evaluate our proposals objectively. On the one hand it's great to have such blind confidence. You are blissfully unaware of all the potential hurdles that your business could encounter and this is giving you the courage and determination to drive your ideas forward. On the other hand, one has to accept that such naivety and lack of experience exposes you to risks which foresight and understanding could help avoid. All this will be very obvious to an investor and you need to be prepared to explain contingency plans and alternative scenarios as comprehensively as you describe your primary plan.

It is worth running a few test presentations before you meet with serious investors. Ask your accountant to quiz you as if he were considering investing his own money. Arrange meetings with practice investors –

albeit investors you don't necessarily want to invest in your business or in front of whom it doesn't really matter if you fail. This exercise will instantly show you where the gaps in your knowledge lie. By evaluating each mock presentation and learning from the experience, you will vastly improve your performance when it comes to delivering the real thing.

Minimise the risks

> **"** a scenario with minimal risk is one where there is proof of a consistent ongoing return on an initial investment **"**

A scenario with minimal risk is one where there is proof of a consistent ongoing return on an initial investment.

In order to strengthen your business proposal, you need to provide firm proof of success. You need to be able to show successful, recurring results on a scale that demonstrates potential for growth. Here is a list of what seem to work as successful risk-reversal tools, in order of perceived preference:

- a track record of perpetual growth and continued sales
- confirmed purchase orders (letters of intent don't count)
- a personal guarantee or matched funding
- positive response rates to marketing campaigns
- testimonials and awards
- referrals.

Please note: A letter from a buyer saying that they like the look of your proposal and could be interested in listing your products in the future is *not* proof that they will definitely buy from you. This is what is known as a letter of intent – it is an indication that they could be interested in buying but real proof can only be found in purchase orders and invoices.

Start gathering small-scale proofs of your success and build these up as an appendix to your business plan. By all means include a letter of intent, but do not be tempted to present this as proof of a buyer's commitment to order.

Funding options

The basic sources of funding for a business venture include:

- commercial lenders
- venture capitalists
- angel investors
- friends and family
- other lenders
- grants and awards.

The type of funding that you will be looking to raise will depend very much on the current needs and position of your business. In the early days, a start-up is often seen as high-risk and of low value. The people who are most likely to invest in you at this stage are the people who know, trust and believe in you. As your business grows and develops, you will be reducing the perceived risk with a proven positive track record and you are much more likely to attract investors who may be less emotionally involved but more inclined to spot a healthy opportunity. Different sources of funding will consequently be more appropriate to the needs of your business at different stages in its growth.

❝ different sources of funding will be more appropriate to the needs of your business at different stages in its growth ❞

As with anything you do, minimise the risks by starting on a small scale. Raise enough funding to further substantiate the growth potential for your business and then leverage this evidence to improve the ratio between the risks associated with your business and the potential for high rewards. Doing so will also improve the value of your proposition.

Commercial lenders

It is not actually the job of commercial lenders such as banks and building societies to invest in any start-up business. Banks are not supposed to invest in businesses – indeed, they are strictly limited in this by the banking laws as this is putting bank depositors' money at risk. Commercial lenders, on the other hand, can be great at financing the cash flow of a business and regularly make loans to small businesses backed by the company's stock debtors.

Successfully borrowing from a bank boils down to finding the right bank manager and this can mean going to visit a fair few. A bank will lend you money when the manager likes and trusts you and your business proposition. So ... you know the rule. If at first you don't succeed, optimise your proposal and go and find another bank and manager.

Venture capital

Venture capital is capital provided by venture capitalists as part of their business strategy. Venture capitalists are professional individuals who have been appointed with the responsibility of investing other people's money for profit. Commonly, a venture capitalist will seek out opportunities that produce a minimum tenfold return over 3 years. They operate on harsh risk/reward ratios and are usually very dismissive of early start-ups. Your chances of receiving venture capital investment will be greatly increased if you are offering a strong product to a stable, sizeable and expanding market and have a proven and reputable management team on board.

While the door to venture capital is more often than not closed to the start-up business owner, smaller private investors are much more receptive to such opportunities.

Angel investors

Smaller private investors commonly known as 'angel' (or 'dragon') investors can be found wherever there is money. These are wealthy individuals interested in making a private placement investment in your business. They are constantly looking for new opportunities. Some will even advertise themselves by joining networks and online groups specifically for angel investors looking for opportunities. Meet-up, LinkedIn and even Facebook has groups for people in this position. They are sharp, efficient and they've seen it all a hundred times before.

You cannot possibly attempt to fool these people. If you are looking to attract their attention, it might be worth your while browsing some of the forums and networking groups first so that you can begin to understand their mentality. You should be acutely aware of the fact that these people will be looking to invest their own hard-earned cash. You need to provide them with accurate facts, figures and data if you wish to improve your chances of getting such wealthy individuals to invest their children's inheritance in your business.

> 66 nobody invests in a business plan. People invest in a company, a product or a person 99

Some of the reasons why they might choose to invest in you are:

- They are going to enjoy watching your business grow and expand and they will feel real personal involvement in your story.
- They have contacts and industry know-how which they believe will dramatically increase your chances of success.
- They are going to reap the rewards of having risked their investment when stakes in your company were relatively cheap.
- Their children, business colleagues and friends will acknowledge and respect the sound decision they made spotting such an early opportunity with you. Equally, if you fail, their decision to invest in you will be taken as a personal failure. You need to be aware of this.

Most private investors are looking to make an investment that either brings synergy to their existing business or has something to do with what they enjoy or feel passionate about. Naturally, they also hope that their investment will generate a hefty return. As with the banks, finding the right investors is all about building relationships. People will either like you and your business or they won't. It's as simple as that.

Please note: You too should consider the value of such relationships. You are inviting somebody into your business. You are going to have to work with these individuals in the future and your working relationship with them should definitely come into consideration. Remember that you always have the option of turning down the wrong investor if you know that you can live and sustain your life with your bread-and-butter income.

Often decisions by investors are made quickly and with a sense of educated 'gut-feeling'. In this instance, their judgement will in all likelihood be formed of two key contributing factors: your attitude and your appearance. Smarten up and look the part. Have a positive and purposeful attitude and approach people in a manner that is appropriate to them.

Friends and family

If you are considering approaching friends and family for capital then be clear about exactly how much money you need and be aware that this money is at risk. Make sure that anyone investing in you also understands this and consider accepting capital only from individuals who can afford to take the risk.

If your parents, siblings, cousins, good friends and in-laws are prepared to invest in your business then they are paying you a massive compliment.

Make sure that you appreciate the personal responsibility that this entails and make it clear to them too. If things start to go wrong then you are going to want to have the support of your friends and family.

Other lenders

A word of warning: be wary of the sharks.

If you are looking for a loan, it can be a good idea to try fundraising from some alternative sources too. In the same way as if you were asking for a mortgage, a lender will in all likelihood ask you what percentage of the total amount you are investing yourself – what your deposit is, so to speak. If you have already raised an amount from another source, you may be able to use this against a further loan from a bank or lender.

A lender may also ask you for a personal guarantee. This is where they ask you to personally guarantee and accept liability for the money they lend you or to put your house up against the loan insurance. Be very wary of this and only attempt it if you know that you can afford the risk. You will find that putting yourself in a position of extreme personal risk can add so much pressure to your situation that when times are tough you are unable to make rational choices and decisions. Being personally at high risk is not a good idea.

Be realistic about when you are likely to pay a loan back.

Grants and awards

Grants for education, innovation and development are awarded in a number of ways. They may be offered as government incentives or provided by large corporations as social or economic responsibility direct-ives. A thorough search online should reveal a number of different oppor-tunities currently open for application.

❝ it may be in your interest to raise the amount you need through a combination of different sources ❞

Applying for grants and awards often involves completing long-winded application forms and can be a time-consuming process. Nonetheless, it is an avenue that is worth exploring. Find out more about your options and remember to read the fine print.

Remember: You are not confined to raising funds from a single source. As with so many things, it may be in your interest to explore a number of alternatives and to raise the amount you need through a combination of different sources.

A winning proposal

A winning proposal is not necessarily the same as your formal business plan. Of course, you need to have written your business plan and established all of your financial forecasts in order to be able to present a winning proposal, but your actual presentation, whether verbal or written, should be a summary of your intentions that will entice an investor into wanting to know more.

Start by telling them the value of your company to date, the amount of money you are looking to raise, the value you intend to generate over the next five years and what this means in terms of a return on any investment. Next reveal the details of your plans.

In your opening sentence you are looking to grab their attention. Use a strong headline and follow this with a clear and focused first paragraph which will hold their interest. It is essential that you immediately give a good impression. You need people to sit up and pay attention. Your aim is to get them wanting to know more.

Your next job is going to be to retain their interest and this is where it is important that you share your story. Don't make it hard work for people to identify the key facts and important information. Disclose all details clearly and up-front. Reveal details about the assets of the business, your customer list, the strength of your intellectual property. You need to be precise and specific about the details you give.

If you have done the exercise on business planning then you will have identified the average lifetime value of each of your customers. If you haven't done this yet, it is essential you do so before you begin contacting investors and lenders. Turn to Chapter 6 for guidelines on how to do this – and do it now. The types of questions that you are likely to be asked are as follows – try to prepare strong answers in advance.

- What is the size of your existing customer list and what is the size of the market?
- Is it a growing or shrinking market?
- How do you propose taking your share of it and what makes you qualified to achieve this task?

- How do you intend to grow your most valuable asset?
- How many customers do you need to attract to break even? How many customers are currently in your sales pipeline and how many customers do you need to attract to really start hitting the big numbers?
- How many products have you sold to date and what plans do you have to sell more in the future?
- How quickly can you produce more products and how will this affect your overheads?
- What are your overheads?
- What is your current income?
- What has the feedback on the product been like?
- Can you expand your sales by growing your customer base and expanding your product range?

At this stage, investors are not really interested in the actual ins and outs of your brilliant brainwave – they are more concerned with weighing up how safe their investment is going to be. Investors and lenders want to know about numbers. Give them a clear overview of the features and benefits behind your idea but avoid letting your passion for your product distract you from the purpose of your presentation.

- How much does the product cost to produce and what can you sell it for – what are your profit margins?
- What are your proposed marketing plans?
- What are your current response rates?

The more detail you know and understand, the better and more confidently you will deliver your presentation. The more you have explored contingency plans and alternative routes to market which would work without the need for investment, the more readily an investor is likely to rise to your opportunity.

Be prepared for all eventualities

If you have fully captured the attention of your audience, retained their interest and stimulated their desire, you must assume that they have understood the potential of this investment in terms of its high rewards. At this point, ask for your investment confidently and succinctly. Then remain silent and wait for their answer.

Try to avoid a one-way presentation. Engage your audience in a dialogue and try to overcome any objections before you draw your presentation towards its closing offer. Having heard all that your potential investors have to say, follow up your conversation with a letter or e-mail inviting them to come back to you with further considerations.

> **❝ grab their attention, retain their interest, stimulate their desire and then call them into action ❞**

Much of what I have explained above is also the same message-delivery method you should adopt when communicating your business plans as a written proposal: grab their attention, retain their interest, stimulate their desire and then call them into action.

One of the most effective ways of calling an investor into action is to present a bandwagon. What I mean by this is that it can be a good idea to create a scenario where, metaphorically, the boat is leaving the harbour and, if they don't jump on board now, they are going to miss the ride.

Investors, lenders and anyone who is being asked to take a risk on your business can be terrible procrastinators and the truth of the matter is that, the longer they procrastinate, the worse things are likely to get for you. Avoid that desperate position by preventing procrastination from going on for too long. Set a deadline or stimulate a scenario that means you are going ahead with this venture with or without them and then stick to your plan. Waiting for others to make decisions outside of your control can be a huge waste of time for any business owner. Don't allow other people's procrastination to put you off your track. You can afford to be firm and friendly.

Present your proposal clearly, concisely and confidently: Go for it! And, if at first you don't succeed, try, try and try again until you do. There are plenty of people out there looking to back the next winner.

signposts to success

- If you want an alternative way to **leverage limited resources** to your maximum advantage – i.e. to develop your ideas on a shoestring – turn to page 26.

- If you want to explore the options that are available to you to **generate an income** from your IP – turn to page 81.

- If further funding will allow you to **put your ideas into production** and you want to find out how best to do this – turn to page 92.

- If you need to **sharpen your presentation skills** before meeting potential funders – turn to page 112.

- If you decide to file your **intellectual property rights** – turn to page 36.

How to get rich from your ideas

Riches from IP

Let's start by asking the question: are you simply an ideas person or are you an entrepreneur? With a little luck you are a creative entrepreneur, in which case, you are in line to make some BIG MONEY. But before we proceed – how do you feel about this? Are you in the game of starting a business to make BIG MONEY or are you innovating and generating new ideas simply because it is your hobby or because it rewards you in other ways?

There is absolutely nothing wrong with doing something purely because you enjoy doing it. There is absolutely every reason why the world needs more social entrepreneurs and if you are in the inventing game solely because you believe you are capable of adding value to the lives of many others through your ideas, then you have my utmost respect.

Here in the UK we seem very uncomfortable with the concept of making BIG MONEY and yet, if we are honest with ourselves, the concept of infinite riches seems to be what stimulates and motivates most of us almost every day. If you wish to substitute the words 'become infinitely wealthy' for 'get rich' in the title of this chapter, then go ahead. It is not for me to choose your destiny or the path of your adventure. This is your journey and your ultimate destination. In this section, we will deal with the possible ways to obtain unlimited wealth from your idea.

ff your ultimate goal is to become filthy rich and infinitely wealthy from the intellectual property you have secured JJ

So, what are your options?

I am going to start by giving you a general overview of the options available to you, if you choose to become wealthy from the intellectual property that you have secured. Having done this, I am then going to take the opportunity to pass personal judgement on each of your options and explain why I believe that you could find yourself chasing rainbows unless you take definitive action towards your ultimate goal. So, just to be clear and for the purpose of this section of the book: **your ultimate goal is to become filthy rich and infinitely wealthy from the intellectual property you have secured.**

In order to do so, you have really only got 3 options:

1 You could sell your intellectual property for a small fortune.

2 You could license your intellectual property and generate a stream of royalty income.

3 You could sell products produced according to your intellectual property and make a healthy profit margin by return.

Selling or transferring the ownership of IP

This is quite simply where you agree to transfer or sell, in part or whole, the ownership of your intellectual property rights to somebody else. The process of doing so is referred to as assignment, whereby you legally assign ownership. You will need to exchange a formal assignment document clearly outlining the terms and conditions of assignment and terms of sale.

Five reasons why you might want to sell or transfer your IP

- **It's worth a fortune** and you want to cash in ... You deserve it!

- **Collaborative development:** You have developed your IP to the limits of your ability and now it is time for somebody else to take over.

- **To recover your investment:** Developing IP can be costly; the sale of it may give you a return on your investment.

- **Company merger or change of ownership:** You may be exiting the company you created and leaving your IP rights under new ownership or your company may merge, at which point the IP rights may be transferred to the new corporation.

- **Your IP is subject to compulsory acquisition:** As with physical property, most governments retain the rights to the compulsory acquisition of your IP.

The sale or transfer of IP ownership is a permanent decision. You should make it with careful consideration. If you have been made an offer for the sale of your IP then do not procrastinate for too long – be sure to listen to your gut feeling when making a time-pressured decision.

How to sell or transfer your IP

❝ the sale or transfer of IP ownership is a permanent decision. You should make it with careful consideration ❞

In order to transfer or sell your intellectual property rights you need to have established the value of your IP and then found a buyer willing to pay this amount. Next you will have to agree the terms and conditions of the sale or transfer and set a date when this exchange will take place.

Upon exchanging, you will notify the relevant office with which your intellectual property rights are lodged of this transfer of ownership. In the UK this would be the Intellectual Property Office and the form you would need to complete is Patents Form 21. This will enable the register of patents to be updated.

Licensing your IP

Licensing your intellectual property means granting somebody else permission to carry out activities which would otherwise be considered an infringement of your intellectual property rights. The person who owns the IP (even under licence you still remain the owner of your IP) and is granting the licence is called the licensor, and the person or company to whom the licence is being granted, is called the licensee.

The agreement that exists between the licensor and the licensee – the parties – is referred to as a **licence agreement** and, in the case of the licence of IP for a physical product: a manufacturing licence agreement. The terms and conditions of such agreements vary enormously and I strongly advise that you seek professional legal help here. So much of the outcome will depend on the negotiations that take place between you and the licensee. You will be more likely to obtain favourable terms if you can prove the value of your IP by quantifying the demand for your product or service in the market and demonstrating the potential for growth.

Five reasons why you might want to license your IP

- **To share the risk:** You are entering new markets where growth can be costly and you are unsure of the potential return from your IP. Licensing it prevents you from absorbing all of the risks. Equally, the licensee has the right to use your IP without the expense and risk associated with research and development.

- **To generate revenue:** If you are already commercialising your IP then you may wish to create an alternative revenue stream by licensing the rights to your IP in a different field.

- **Increased market scope:** If by licensing your IP you are actually joining forces with someone who has access to markets that are otherwise beyond your reach, you will increase your market scope and opportunity. The licensee will obtain a competitive advantage in the market and scope for greater gain.

- **To reduce time and costs:** The expertise of the licensee and fast routes to market will save you time and resources. While from the licensee's point of view, the concept of buying in innovation reduces the costs and time of in-house development.

- **Collaboration:** Negotiating a licence agreement is more than just agreeing the terms and conditions that apply. You are effectively forming a partnership. Working together will increase productivity; you will develop further IP faster and more effectively; you will better understand the market and you will grow exponentially as a result.

> **❝ think of a license agreement as being like a marriage; take your time before getting involved ❞**

Think of a license agreement as being like a marriage; take your time before getting involved.

How to license your IP

Before you can license your intellectual property at the value you believe it is worth, you need to be able to prove or at least identify its actual worth – this will help you with your negotiations later on.

Having established the value of your IP, you need to find a willing licensee. As with selling IP, the more you can create a demand for what you have to offer, the stronger your powers of negotiation will be.

Make sure you have what lots of people want. Be clear on the ownership of intellectual property rights and be sure to have secured your own.

Next you need to negotiate the terms that best suit you and your IP. It is a good idea to get the licensee to sign a confidentiality agreement at this stage. In that way you are free to discuss confidential and non-confidential information during the negotiations.

Finally, and dependent on the structure of your agreement, you will need to conduct due diligence checks and oversee the terms of the agreement. It

❝ familiarise yourself with a few licence agreements before attempting to negotiate one for the first time ❞

is always a good idea to familiarise yourself with a few licence agreements before attempting to negotiate one for the first time. Whenever you buy a copy of software you usually receive an IP licence, you will also find plenty to review online.

Points for consideration in a licence agreement

Parties	Who is the agreement between?
	• Name, company number (if applicable) and registered address of the licensor.
	• Name, company number (if applicable) and registered address of the licensee?
	Are any third parties to be involved – subsidiaries or partner groups for instance?
Grant of licence	What is the main IP being licensed?
	Has this IP been secured?
	Is any third-party intellectual property to be used in conjunction with the main IP?
	What knowledge and know-how, confidential material or unregistered intellectual property rights are to be included?
	Is the IP free from any restrictions or liabilities?

▶

Scope of grant	Are you granting an exclusive, a non-exclusive or a sole licence of the IP? • Exclusive (licensor may not use the IP) • Non-exclusive (licensor may use the IP and grant other licences); or • Sole (licensor may use the IP but will not grant other licences) May the licensee grant sub-licences to others?
Restriction and territory	Will the right to use the IP be restricted to a specific territory? Will the right to use the IP be restricted to: • the field of use • the channels of distribution? May the licensee transfer (assign) the licence freely or only with the licensor's permission: • to provide services to others? • to manufacture and sell products? • to import products? • to carry out a process? What rights and restrictions will apply in respect of: • copying works? • modifying/adapting/translating works? • making improvements? • incorporating into another work/with other IP? • publication and distribution? • sharing with others? • using only on/with a specific platform or device? How will improvements be identified? Who will own future IP?
Fees and payment	How will the licensor and licensee each release benefit from the licence? • One or more lump sum payments? • Royalty payment – How is it to be calculated? • Advance on royalty payment? When will payment take place? Will there be guaranteed minimum payments?
IP protection and infringement	Will the licensor or the licensee be responsible for registering any IP, or renewing any existing registration? What is the process for pursuing any infringers?
Confidentiality	What information is to be kept confidential and for how long? Is either party subject to the Freedom of Information Act?

Warranties and liability	Will the licensor give any warranty:
	• as to its ownership of the IP/its right to license?
	• that the licensed IP will not infringe third party rights?
	Will the licensee give:
	• any warranty that the licensed IP/material will comply with quality standards and specification?
	• liability and adequate insurance cover?
Termination	Is the licence:
	• of indefinite duration (for the life of the IP)?
	• for a fixed period (and if it is what is that period)?
	• terminable by either party giving notice to the other?
	Willl the licence be terminable for breach of contract or insolvency of a party or ownership of the licensor?
	What will happen on the termination/expiry of the licence?
	Are any provisions of the licence agreement to continue after termination/expiry and for what period?

Three slippery snakes

1 A licensee may wish to tie you into a licence agreement purely to prevent you or other potential competitors from gaining a competitive edge from your intellectual property but without any real intention of ever launching your IP into the market.

2 You may think that your IP is worth a fortune; convincing the licensee of this might be a different matter. Prove your worth with sales results and a clear route to market.

3 Approaching a potential licensee puts you on the back foot when it comes to negotiations. You are in a much stronger position if you are able to create a demand or a situation that attracts a licensee towards you. The best way to do this is by proving your sales and identifying your route to market.

Commercialising your IP

Commercialising your IP is the process of taking your IP to market yourself so as to generate an income from sales. This is the option that appears to be the hardest work. Generating revenue from the sale of products using your own intellectual property requires setting up production and routes to market; it involves building relationships, opening market channels and closing sales. It involves sales order processing and credit control.

You will need to market and promote your idea, develop new products to add to your range, grow your brand and your business in line with your customers' needs. It is relentless and never-ending but full of scope and opportunity too. **It can be an avenue well worth pursuing.**

Often creative people have an inclination towards off-loading their ideas onto the money-makers and this can be a huge mistake. Creative people have a tendency to see the world differently. The so-called money-makers don't always share this same vision and are often not nearly as well qualified as the original creator can be when it comes to selling and marketing ideas. If a creative person can learn to apply his or her creative thinking to business development and growth strategy, driving ideas to market becomes an exciting and thrilling ride.

Don't dismiss the option of commercialising your own ideas simply because you are petrified by the prospect. You are already demonstrating that you have the attitude it takes and the ability to take plenty of action. You will quickly pick up along the way the skills that you lack.

The pros and cons of all your options

Bear with me here, and excuse my sweeping generalisations – my justification for the following bold statements is sheer bitter experience.

Most inventors jump straight to the conclusion that the easiest way for them to get their product into the market will be to license their intellectual property to an existing industry giant who will launch it globally under one worldwide exclusive agreement and pay out a massive royalty. Isn't this the ultimate dream?

❝ your IP is only really worth the paper that it is written on until you have been able to prove its market value ❞

So, what about the harsh reality? The harsh reality is that in 99.5% of all cases, your intellectual property is only really worth the paper that it is written on until you have been able to **prove its market value.**

If you decide that your preferred method for making money out of your idea is to sell your intellectual property outright, you had better have a good idea of what the piece of paper you are selling is actually worth. More importantly, you need to be in a position to prove this worth to others. Otherwise you will be lucky to get anyone to give you more than a fiver for your 'bits of paper'.

It is sales ledgers and a track record of positive results that will attract a buyer to your IP. Quite simply, the greater your turnover, the more inarguably valuable your bits of paper become. The same applies to licensing. In order to attract the right kind of licence or assignment agreement, you are going to need to prove the worth of your intellectual property. And, to prove the worth of your IP, you are going to need an actual track record of sales.

If your preferred business 'exit strategy' is through the sale of your intellectual property then you need to build up the value of your IP before you start looking for a potential buyer. Think about this like a house. An architect's plans on paper are worth a fraction of the value of an immaculately constructed, luxuriously furnished, beautifully positioned family home finished and ready to occupy – or, better still, a whole new estate of homes like this, all built according to the one original plan. The same goes for your intellectual property – consider your patents, design registrations and copyrights as simply being your architect's plans. To create an easily saleable asset, you've got to build your house (or be prepared to trade in the plans at a fraction of their worth).

To a certain extent, the same principles apply to the licensing of intellectual property – though rather than having built a house, you can perhaps get away with having erected a tent or a scaffolding representation.

In the case of licensing, the licensee is looking for the potential to grow your existing, successful model faster by applying to your project the resources they have at their disposal. Although you might find a licensee who can spot the opportunity you are presenting them on paper, you are much more likely to attract a really great licensing partner if you have got proof (albeit on a smaller scale) of the potential for huge success.

So, the harsh reality of this whole equation is that if you can prove a successful sales track record you are ultimately going to be in a much better position to:

(a) license your intellectual property

(b) sell your intellectual property outright (and at the value you truly deserve)

In essence this boils back down to one simple thing: **You need to put your product or service into small-scale production, test and prove the market potential yourself.**

With the right kind of performance and the right kind of results you may even find that a licensee or potential new owner approaches you, instead of it having to be the other way round. In this instance, you are in a much stronger negotiating position and are more likely to end up with the outcome you want and are entitled to.

By popular demand: an extra word on licensing your intellectual property

As with successfully raising funding for your business, the key to successfully licensing your intellectual property lies in your ability to convince a potential licensee that this has got nothing at all to do with BIG RISK and absolutely everything to do with MASSIVE REWARD.

> **❝ you need to eliminate the perceived risk and prove the potential for massive reward ❞**

And don't forget to put yourself in a position where third parties approach you. Turning up, in classic inventor style, with a brown paper bag under your arm and your thoughts full of the 'next amazing invention' it contains, is *not* a good image. It will also be unlikely to get you the respect you deserve from your audience. However, being invited to a meeting because what you have been achieving has been making a few hungry investors sit up and take notice … well, that's a totally different situation. Make sure they know who you are and how to get hold of you but don't go chasing the ultimate licensing deal!

Acquiring wealth from your IP simply boils down to the amount of action you are prepared to take in order to do so. There is no easy option. Success really does grow from determined and focused hard work.

Good luck and do let me know how you get on!

signposts to success

■ If you decide to take action and commercialise your IP – turn to page 92 (if I was offering advice I'd be suggesting this option).

■ If you want to generate unlimited profits from selling your IP – turn to page 101.

■ If you want to know what to do with all the money that you are currently making – turn to page 154.

■ If you decide that you need to strengthen the value of your IP before proceeding any further – turn to page 36.

9

How to put your brainwave into production

The move into production

Before you go into full-scale production, it is important to test the market. If you would like to know more about how to test the market before you

test the market before you begin full-scale production

begin full-scale production then turn to Chapter 12. If you have tested the market and are happy with the results, this could well be the time to move forward into full-scale production.

This can feel like an insurmountable challenge. Indeed, when you look at the cost implications it might even seem like an impossibility, but believe me when I tell you that **where there is a will there is a way**. The important thing is to find that way. Begin by investigating whether it is possible to start off with batch production with a view to scaling this up at a later date to reach mass-market quantities.

One of the biggest hurdles for any lone individual starting out with an idea is the need to have a production-quality product before you can really begin the sales and marketing stage. Buyers, especially volume buyers, are resistant to risk. They are unlikely to buy a 'concept' from you and will want to see the quality and level of your production capabilities before signing off a large purchase order. What this means is that you need to be in a position where you are holding actual stock before you can begin approaching the larger accounts for sales. If you can find a way of producing your product to the right standard and quality levels without the need to invest in large quantities of stock then so much the better.

Sources of supply

Look for local producers and find standard components

OK, so your design is original. There is nothing else like it available in the market. But how many standard parts are you using and can you alter the design to accommodate more existing components without actually sacrificing any of the features and benefits?

This is a very important question.

> **if you can reduce your tooling costs by using existing components you have already made a saving**

One of the major expenses in investing in new product development is the set-up costs involved in mass-production tooling. If you can reduce your tooling costs by effectively using existing components (components that are made from production tools that exist already) then so much the better – you have already made a saving.

In the instance of the Doctor Cook saucepans, for example, I was not aware of tooling costs (or did not think long and hard enough about them) before going into production. I wasted a considerable amount of money (and time) and had one Malaysian manufacturer laughing their heads off at me – and all the way to bank – in the process.

It was impossible (or so I thought) for me to begin production on a small scale and local production facilities were out of the question due to the cost involved. In order to begin competitively, I was going to have to look at manufacturing in the Far East. What I failed to realise was that half of my product existed already.

Saucepans are common enough and there are plenty of Far Eastern producers making them. I didn't think about the possibility of using existing components – instead, I went ahead and spent a small fortune on new tooling for my design. The truth is, what is original about my design is the handle and the lid knob. The cookware body and the lid itself existed already and these were available in all sorts of shapes, materials, qualities and sizes. It should simply have been a question of making the best choice. But no, I went ahead and invested in tooling for the whole lot.

This was a big mistake – the tooling that I invested in produced a high-end product that the market did not respond positively enough to. I was positioning my product as design-led and high-end when, in essence, my target market was people like my granny.

❝ start by breaking down your design into components and investigate what elements exist already ❞

I don't want you to make the same mistake, so think about it and *test*. Start by breaking down your design into components and investigate what elements exist already. The existing components may not necessarily be used in the same context as your invention, but there is no reason why you can't adapt what exists already to suit your needs.

I recently helped a client of mine develop one of his inventions. This was a revolutionary fish lure, the details of which he is not ready to disclose. The inventor in question was struggling to see how he could afford to build the mechanism needed to create the effect he was after – an innovation that would attract the fish to take his bait. When we started exploring his options, the solution was actually very readily available as a number of different existing components. Sitting on the shop shelves was his solution at a fraction of the cost it would take to develop from scratch.

Remember the brainstorming exercises at the beginning of this book and keep thinking laterally and openly. Make a list of all the different components that make up your product or process. Decide which of them are completely unique to your design and which other parts can be sourced from existing suppliers. For instance, there is absolutely no need for you to invest in a nut and bolt. These exist already in varying diameters. You need to specify which diameter best suits your needs and then design your product or process around this, rather than specifying the diameter of the hole and then needing to tool for a special nut and bolt that fits it. Spending time really considering this exercise will dramatically reduce your costs in tooling.

Next, start looking at where these components are available and think what modifications it is going to take to make them suitable for your design. Consider what process is required to assemble your components and whether it is possible that you could batch produce and assemble your components locally.

One of the most cost-effective ways to manage your business is to produce your products 'just in time' – ideally, once you have already confirmed a purchase order. Being able to take orders in advance and then produce your invention to meet this demand will ensure that you avoid running into cash flow problems. However, you will need production-quality samples from which to generate sales.

Having considered the possibilities of batch production, small-volume production and even local assembly and fabrication, all of which will keep your initial set-up costs down, you may decide that it is simply not a cost-effective option or practicable for your product to be produced in this way. For instance, you may need specialist machinery or raw materials which are expensive in this country. In that case, you will need to start investigating your alternative options.

Find out where your competitors currently produce their products and whether there is a reason for this. It might be that the raw materials you need are only available from one specific source, or that the cost of materials and labour make it more feasible – and consequently more competitive – for you to produce your products in a specific area. Your competitors, especially if they are long-established, mature businesses, will have already worked this one out. It is a good idea to do your research so as to avoid any pitfalls in the future.

If your only option seems to be to produce abroad then don't let this thought worry you. It is becoming increasingly difficult to produce products effectively in the western world and many companies and inventors are very successfully manufacturing their products overseas.

How to recruit the right manufacturer

As with all the big decisions associated with your product, the final call is going to be yours and you will need to do your research and explore the options available to you. Effectively, you will have to interview a series of manufacturers until you are convinced that you have found the one that best suits your needs.

❝ recruiting the wrong manufacturer can cost your business 10 times the invoice you end up paying them ❞

Recruiting the wrong manufacturer can cost your business 10 times the invoice you end up paying them. Take your time making the right decision, the first time.

First and foremost, **do not make your judgement based on the manufacturer's appearance or enthusiasm.** Just because a manufacturer that you talk to absolutely loves your new idea, it does not mean that he or she is going to be the best option for your business. In the same way, a fancy showroom, or being wined and dined in a posh restaurant tells you absolutely nothing about how well this particular manufacturer is going to be able to reproduce your job.

Go prepared to interview them effectively. Ask yourself the following questions to help you compile your 'shopping list':

- What kind of production capabilities are you looking for? An industrial designer or the person who has developed your design for manufacture may be able to help here.
- What sort of machinery does your ideal producer need to have? If you are unsure then you should ask the designer or the person preparing your CAD files to specify a production method list for you. This is a list of all the different types of manufacturing process that will be required to produce your design. Your ideal supplier should have the capacity to carry out all these processes.
- What volume capabilities are you looking for?
- What is the factory's track record?
- Are they able to supply you with references or testimonials? It is always a good idea to speak to one or more of their customers to find out the inside details.
- What sort of quality-controlled fail rates is the factory currently experiencing?
- How often is a product off their production line rejected and what level of quality are they able to guarantee you?
- Are you looking for a guarantee on the product itself?
- What length of production time is acceptable to you?
- What sort of payment terms are you looking for?
- Where do you want your product to be delivered to?

All of these questions should help you write a detailed list of exactly what you want from your ideal factory. The longer your list, the better your chances are of finding what it is you really need.

Remember, manufacturers are business people too. If your business does well, their business will also benefit. Because of this, you may be able to negotiate some sort of start-up or shared-risk agreement whereby they will fund some of the initial start-up costs (developing new tooling, etc) in return for quantities of guaranteed orders. You may decide, however, that you prefer the autonomy of owning your own tooling. Either way, make sure that you agree with the producer under what terms the tooling will be used and whether you have the right to move it to another supplier should the need arise.

Once you have written a comprehensive 'shopping list' for your ideal factory, you can begin your search. There are a number of agencies and advisory boards that can often help you find different producers and exporters.

- Most countries have a government department responsible for trade and industry – in the UK it is the Department for Business, Innovation and Skills – and it can be a good idea to begin by contacting your local representative. They may well be able to put you in touch with or recommend producers in the specific areas that you are targeting.
- Alibaba is a great online resource specifically designed to allow you to search for manufacturers of specific products and components.
- In the UK, the government organisation MAS (Manufacturing Advisory Service) may well be able to point you in the right direction too.

It is a good idea to shortlist at least 5 producers for a detailed inspection. You or somebody within your organisation should definitely consider visiting each of the factories on your shortlist and judging them against a comparative standard.

Only once you have done all of your homework should you start thinking about disclosing your invention and then only under a non-disclosure agreement.

Security and protection

Sending your products to be manufactured abroad can seem like a daunting process and one which is out of your control. With the advent of new technologies and better international communications, this need not be the case, but it is advisable to take precautions.

China has always had the reputation of being amazing at copying other people's ideas. If you are an inventor, this is obviously going to cause you huge concern. A lot is being done by the Chinese government to patrol

❝ there are steps you can take to ensure that your IP is respected by the people who are making your product for you ❞

the infringement of intellectual property rights and producers globally are better educated about what this entails and the perils of using IP without the owner's permission. There are still a few steps you can take to ensure that your intellectual property is respected by the people who are making your product for you.

Consider which of the following is a feasible option for you:

- **Sticking a hologram of authenticity on the product or packaging.** Effectively, you supply the producer with a hologram sticker which they then attach to the product on your behalf. This allows you to count how many products are being produced against how many stickers you are supplying. If you come across one of your products that does not have a sticker on it, you will know that the factory is supplying other distributors through the back door. Psychologically, holograms of authenticity can have a very good impact on the producer and they may also help to add value to the marketing of your invention.

- **Manufacture original components in separate sources** and have an independent party complete the assembly process. In this way, not everyone in the loop is fully aware of what the rest of the process entails, making it harder for any one producer to copy your concept in its entirety. Logistically, this approach can provide you with a few extra headaches. Be sure to keep the process as simple as possible and only really try to 'hide' components that are critical to your original concept.

- **Introducing a 'secret recipe' or 'special formula'** – say, a protective coating or surface finish – that you deliver to the producer directly and don't tell them how it is made. In this way, the producer is only able to finish your product with your secret ingredient; you will know how much of this ingredient you have supplied and, consequently, how many products should have been produced. You can then reconcile these figures against the manufacturing log book, which will show how often your tooling has been used. If the tooling has been used more often than the quantities of secret ingredient should allow, you know that something is wrong and can take action to rectify it.

■ **Conduct regular quality inspection visits** and have quality-control inspectors turn up unannounced. No producer will like you doing this, but there is absolutely no reason why you can't. If the factory is not welcoming to your inspector then perhaps this is because they have something to hide.

■ **Go and see the factory yourself** at least once and build a relationship with the owner. People at the end of the day deal with people. If you have a healthy relationship with the producers of your product then this might deter them from effectively stealing straight out of your back pocket. Do be warned, however – not everyone's smile means the same thing. You'll just have to trust your instinct on that one.

■ **Have the factory sign a confidentiality agreement** before you reveal the details of your design. This is essential. If a factory is unwilling to sign such a document you have serious cause to ask why.

■ **Have a production agreement in place** between you and the factory. If you are dealing with a producer abroad then keep this agreement as simple as possible. Use easy-to-understand, simple English and make sure that the agreement is governed under the laws of your home country.

❝ if you are in doubt, seek expert advice: manufacturing agents deal daily with the problems you are facing ❞

Finally, if you are at all in doubt, seek expert advice. There are a number of different manufacturing agents and people who deal daily with the problems you are facing. You may well be able to find an agent willing to work on your behalf and happy to share a percentage of the profits when the sales start to come through. Search for such individuals online. Many of them have UK as well as foreign offices. Industry associations or the Manufacturing Advisory Service (MAS) may well be able to advise you but always remember to check out any agents or seek reputable referrals before making any conclusive decisions.

Remember: be sceptical about paying anyone too much money up-front. At this stage in your business **cash is king** and you don't want to be giving it away unnecessarily. Use the same due diligence to select a manufacturing agent as you would in choosing the manufacturer themselves.

The best way to put your brainwave into production is to take action and do it. As you make steps in the right direction the overall route will become clearer. Start talking to manufacturers, exporters and agents. Ask them questions. Much of the advice they give you will be free of charge, and the more you learn, the quicker and easier it will become for you to make the right decision.

signposts to success

- If you want to improve your ability to sell and market your ideas – turn to page 101.

- If you need to develop your idea further in readiness for production – turn to page 26.

- If you are concerned about possible infringement or want to know more about what you can do to stop somebody from copying your ideas – turn to page 135.

10

How to generate unlimited profits from sales

Issues in communication

In my opinion, your attititude to selling is one of the most significant milestones in establishing how far along the road from brainwave to business you have travelled. As innovators, creators and ideas people, we tend to hate the concept of 'selling' our ideas; as entrepreneurs this is one of our favourite jobs! If you hate the idea of going out there and selling your product or service then here is some really exciting news for you. If you still feel that the 'sales part' is just not your job then this is one really quick lesson which will totally alter your mindset and set you on the fast track to success. If you love selling, then congratulations! You are well on your way to success. Read the following pages and refresh the skills you are already perfecting.

❝ all successful entrepreneurs are incredibly talented salespeople. As the creator of your concept, so are you ❞

All successful entrepreneurs are incredibly talented salespeople. As the creator of your concept, so are you! You, above all other people, know more about your idea than you could ever reasonably train somebody else to know and you are passionate about what it is you have to offer. You care about your concept, you care about the benefit that this offers to society and you know that what you have created is a better solution than anything else that is currently available in the market. This makes the job of selling your offering a whole lot easier.

When I first started out as a designer, peddling my 'brown paper bag', my secret idea, my life-changing invention, I found the whole concept of selling distasteful. How could I, in all honesty, go out there and tell people what a brilliant concept I had come up with and how I had managed to answer an age-old problem by simply applying innovative thought. I had won awards; I was brilliant; my idea was even better and I was going to change the world with it ... The thought of actually voicing all this out loud horrified me. I, I, I ... I've never been one to enjoy boasting about my personal achievements and the idea of standing in front of an audience explaining my brilliance out loud ... Well, it just didn't feel right.

And then it dawned on me. This had absolutely nothing to do with me. **In fact it has everything to do with you (the customer).** By understanding **you**, by taking the time to get to know **you**, what it is that **you** love and live for, what problems **you** face and what needs **you** have as a result, I was able to offer **you** a solution, an answer to **your** problems and something which would enhance **your** life. As soon as I realised that this had nothing to do with me and absolutely everything to do with you ... well, let's just say, my sales figures shot up and I really started to enjoy the process.

You are offering somebody an answer to their problems. You are enhancing somebody's life; you are saving them time, energy, hassle or concern by making life safer, easier and more enjoyable and beneficial. They are going to thank you for this, not resent you. You should be proud of what you have to offer, proud of the fact that you are providing them with a product or service that answers their needs so well.

> ❝ selling is all about identifying somebody's needs and offering them the solution ❞

Selling is all about identifying somebody's needs and offering them the solution – ideally, right when they need it most. How much better will you feel about the sales process when you realise that, by selling your idea to somebody, you are actually doing them a huge favour by solving their problems?

Understanding your customers

Sales is all about understanding the psychology of how people purchase: how and when they are ready to buy. To sell successfully you must understand the needs and desires of your customers. Once you have truly understood what somebody needs or what they want, it is just a simple question of supplying it to them.

Gone is the era of clever close techniques and complicated strategies. Today it's all about consultative selling: becoming a consultant – a sales consultant – to your customers. You are the expert and they are coming to you for advice. Your customers are looking for your leadership and guidance in how to best meet their needs. They are effectively hiring you to act as a consultant on their behalf. In approaching you, they have chosen to buy; your job now is to establish what it is that they need and how much they value it.

Establishing someone's needs is about asking them questions. People love talking about themselves and the more you can encourage them to do so, the easier your job as a 'consultant' will be.

Who, what, where, when, why and how?

Ask them who they are shopping for, what they are looking for, and where they intend to use it. If they say they want to use it in the caravan, for example, you'll be thinking about their need for storage. The reply: 'At my daughter's wedding' might get you thinking along different lines. Ask more questions: 'Why do you need it?' 'How many special features would you like to have?' 'How often will you be using it?' The more you ask, the better equipped you will be to provide them with exactly what it is that they want.

Once you have established your customer's primary needs, you need to understand what it is about these needs that they value. You know your product or service like the back of your hand; understanding your customers' needs and desires will help you position your product presentation. Do they value safety? Do they value practicality or aesthetic design? What concerns them? What are their loves and dislikes? Gauge these on a scale of value or importance – how important is it to them? Very rarely is this about price.

Having established what your customer needs, a good question to ask is simply 'What would be most important to you about (... your needs)?' For the sake of argument, please allow me to use my own example: cookware. 'What would be most important to you about (your cookware)?' Their answer will tell you what it is they value most: 'I must be able to use it in the dishwasher' or 'It needs to be relatively lightweight – I struggle to lift the heavier pans but I do like a good cooking surface, something with a good base'. These answers give you an indication of what your customer values. Another good question is: 'What is it that you value most about your current (cookware)?' Listen to the answers here. 'Is there anything that you dislike about your current saucepans?' Answers to any of these questions will give you angles from which to approach the presentation of your own offering.

As you uncover more and more information about your customer's needs and the value they assign to these, you should begin to evaluate their willingness to buy by asking them leading questions. Here is a really good question to ask at this stage: 'How will you know when you've found a ...? To use my example: 'How will you know when you've found a (piece of cookware) that truly' – and then you pick out the most important value of all – 'fits in your caravan?' 'How will you know when you have found a piece of cookware that really is best suited to your caravan?' or 'How will you know when you have found a piece of cookware that has a great conductive base plate and is still lightweight and easy to handle?'

What is your customer's response here likely to be? They're going to say: 'It will feel right', 'I'll just know it', 'I will know it when I see it'. They are actually going to have an emotional response. By asking them this question you are, in essence, asking them to imagine for just one split second exactly what it will feel like to own the product or service you are about to offer them.

Really it makes very little difference who you are selling to, whether you are selling to a consumer, selling business to business or selling your business to a group of investors. The techniques are very much the same. You are speaking to people irrespective of their position. Just as you might change the tone and temper of your language when you are speaking with friends compared to work colleagues or potential new customers, so will you need to modify the tone, temper and delivery of your sales pitch to make it appropriate and relevant to your audience.

Rapport and communication

Making a successful sale is all about rapport. The better the rapport you have with your customers, the better your performance as a salesperson will be. You've got to make your customer feel good around you. The better your customer feels, the easier the process of selling will become. In short, you and your customers have got to click. If you're not feeling the love, so to speak, for the people you are effectively engaging in a sales consultation then ... well, ask yourself why that is. Great sales is all about great communication.

Remember, you are acting as your customer's sales consultant, establishing their needs and how much they value these. The better the rapport you have with your customers, the happier they will be to share information with you.

Search for a similarity between you and them. Find things which connect you or things that you have in common. Do you have children the same age? Do you share the same hobbies or interests? Have you been to the same place on holiday? Do you live in the same neighbourhood or enjoy similar music? Ask them questions to understand what motivates and inspires them, what pains or troubles them, what they need and how you can help.

People really connect on two levels. They connect through **pleasure** – shared enjoyments – but they also connect through **pain** and this is important to remember. Two people who have broken their wrists, for instance, will compare and share experiences. Two people who have shared similar sadness will also bond. If you can connect with your customer by sharing and understanding their pain then you are likely to form a strong bond.

If you can't find connections and similarities naturally then you can try to create them. Have you come across the mirror and match sales technique? This is a great way to make people feel comfortable around you. Mirror and match your customer's body language and mannerisms; look to follow the tone and patterns in their voice. If they talk quietly and slowly, you should do the same. If they are louder and more boisterous, then you too should look to raise the pace and tone of your voice. This is not a question of an amateur dramatics class; it has got to be much more subtle and natural than that. Try mirroring and matching their body position: simply cross your arms the same way they do or shift your weight onto one foot; mirror gestures; match the speed of their movements. You can even synchronise your own breathing to match theirs. Obviously, you can mirror the volume of their voice and the speed of their speech, but what about the type of language they use? What about the pauses and the pace of their dialogue? Look to emulate them subtly and naturally and try to find points through which you can both connect.

❛❛ to understand your customer's needs and their values well you need to be a really effective and highly flexible communicator ❜❜

To understand your customer's needs and their values well you need to be a really effective and highly flexible communicator. You need to accommodate your customer; you need to adapt to make them feel comfortable and at ease in your presence. You need to connect with them and form a bond of mutual trust and respect. Mirror and match the tone of voice, body language, mannerisms and movements. Make others enjoy your company and welcome your insights into their needs. Once you have achieved this, presenting your customer with the solution to their problems will be a very easy and rewarding task for you to do.

Identify the decision-maker

Successful sales come from qualified leads. A sales lead is someone who could potentially buy your product. A qualified lead is someone who has the capacity, ability and interest in making a purchase from you.

You need to qualify, or test, how sure the people you are targeting are about doing business with you. You've got to decide if they are worth the effort. There is nothing more frustrating than spending hours finding out the needs and values of somebody who is not the decision-maker or who is not qualified to make a purchase from you. Pre-qualifying your sales leads can save you a lot of time and make your overall sales strategy much more effective and successful. You've got to establish if you are talking to the right person and again, the easiest way to do this is by asking questions.

If you need to establish whether the person to whom you are talking is really the decision maker or whether you need to be talking to somebody higher up the chain, a good question to ask is: 'Will anybody else be involved in the purchasing process?' You have effectively got to ask them if they qualify as someone who will benefit from your consultation services. For instance, using my cookware example: 'If we find a range of cookware that you can use in the dishwasher but that will also fit in your caravan and is easy to handle, who else will need to be involved in the decision-making process? Will your wife take an interest?'

> **❝ it is a really good idea to get all decision-makers involved in the purchasing process ❞**

It is a really good idea to get all decision-makers involved in the purchasing process. Inviting everybody to participate in one conversation firstly saves you having to repeat yourself but, more importantly saves your lead from having to relay your sales presentation to the decision-maker. Naturally, you would prefer to have this conversation yourself, especially as you really begin to refine your skills and sales process.

The cycle of understanding

One thing that is really important to realise at this stage is that the sales process is *not* a big build-up to the close. The close is the point of actual sale – however, the sales process is a cycle of understanding between you and your lead. Of course, you hope that the outcome of the process is a successful sale but throughout the cycle – a cycle which you should continue to evolve until you either close the sale or get told to go away by your lead – you must continually be testing your customer's readiness to buy. This is referred to as the **pre-close**. Testing with a pre-close question will give you an indication of how well on track you are and how close your customer is to being ready to buy.

Say things like 'That's a good price, isn't it?' or 'It's guaranteed to be safer and easier than (traditional cookware) – that's important, don't you think?' or be more direct 'It's a great idea that will make a real difference to you, won't it?' A 'yes' answer to any of these types of question tells you that you are right on track and your customer is ready to let you offer them the sale. If you get a slight hesitation or even a 'No' then embrace this by asking them more questions.

Overcoming objections

In order to overcome an objection, it is important to understand exactly what this objection is. What is concerning your customer enough for them to hesitate or disagree? What is it about your offering that doesn't quite meet their needs?

This hesitation is telling you that, at some point during the cycle of understanding, you have failed to assign value to your customer's needs accurately enough. You should seek out hints of negativity such as these. Listen and understand where the hesitation stems from. Ask: 'Why do you feel that?', 'What is it that concerns you about … (their objection)?' Once you've understood what it is that your customer objects to, repeat this back to them to be sure. Realign this in order of their valued priorities: 'I understand that you are not comfortable with the stainless steel body. However, you did mention that you wanted something that was dishwasher-proof. What else would you like your cookware to be able to do?' This puts you right back to re-establishing their needs and values by asking more questions.

If you encounter objections about price then, nine times out of ten, this is because you have not successfully communicated the value of what you are offering. Re-associate the price tag with their very first need or most highly valued priority, whether this was safety, style or design, a need for easy storage – or for a particular use. Re-establish what this was and how much value they attributed to it: 'You said that you were struggling with the weight of your old pans but that you didn't want to compromise on the cooking surface. The encapsulated aluminum base will give you a really even and rapid transfer of heat across the entire base and you'll find this new design very easy to handle.'

Parallel the price to the cost of not purchasing your product. In the case of my cookware: 'How much would it cost you if you had to take time off work because of a repetitive strain injury?' 'How much would it cost you if something went wrong because you didn't own my brilliant innovation?' Eliminate the risks associated with purchasing your offering by exposing what the risks could be should the customer decide not to buy your product or service.

You can always use testimonials to support your claims: 'So and so, who came in yesterday, has just bought the 28cm stir-fry pan. She said she just loved her milk jug and seemed to use the saucepan every day.' Testimonials can be a really effective support tool to any sales presentation. Always remember to collect testimonials from your regular customers and to ask returning customers what they thought of their purchase. Ask them if they would mind you using what they have just said as part of your sales presentation. You'll find they'll be delighted!

Asking for the sale

A very important aspect of selling is the infamous **close**: getting the commitment for your customer to buy your product; actually asking your qualified sales lead to part with their hard-earned cash and closing the deal. Never ever assume that, just because you have brilliantly identified your customers' needs, ingeniously and accurately attributed value to these needs and desires and then presented the perfect product in an Oscar-winning performance, they are automatically going to make the decision to buy from you. You have got to ask for them for the sale. You have got to ask for the close.

If you've got a tendency to get nervous at this point, to hesitate or procrastinate, then you must get over this. I mean that. Do more than get over it. Become proud that you are able to sell your product. In your role as a consultant, you are offering your customer a solution – a solution to their very real, perhaps even painful problem. You are offering them something which will enhance and enrich their lives and you should be proud of doing so, not chewing pen ends or shifting your weight from foot to foot. You should be happy and embracing, welcoming, if not even a little relieved. All along, you have led your customer to this point. In acting as a consultant, you have established their needs and you now understand what is important to them. You have guided them successfully and safely – maybe even enjoyably – through the sales journey, and if you've done your job properly, then they will be thanking you for it. You should be proud.

Humans are funny creatures. We actually enjoy the security of being led: having somebody in the know, as it were, tell us what to do, or someone who we trust guide our way. Understanding that people actually want to be led and knowing how to take them to where they want to go makes you an outstanding member of any organisation and, as a salesperson, a peak performer.

Every single thing you do and say needs to convey certainty and confidence. You know more about your subject that they do and you are here to guide them in trust, to where they want to go. Right from the word go you know they want to buy. You must assume that they want there to be a sale. Your customer wants to buy, now it is just a question of what. Once you have got them to the stage of the close you will actually find, assuming you've done a good job, that this is the easy part. Simply ask them for the sale: 'May I sell you this product?' Directly and specifically ask them to buy your product. And then shut up. Say nothing and listen. If you do meet with an objection at this stage then the sales cycle just continues.

Remember: 'No' simply means 'Not right now' or 'No, I've not fully understood yet' or 'No, I need to get somebody else involved in making this decision.' It very rarely means 'No, I will never consider purchasing your product.' It is your job to understand what 'No' really means.

So, keep confident, be assertive, offer certainty in your role as a leader and directly, specifically ask for the sale.

The PAS technique

The PAS technique is a fabulous way to present a new and ingenious idea, especially when you have developed it to solve a genuine problem! PAS stands for Problem, Agitate and Solve. Present the problem, agitate this problem until your customer has fully understood or got to a point when they can either directly or indirectly – through personal experience or the experience of friends and family – relate to this problem and then, quite simply, present the solution. This technique works brilliantly for many different products but it works particularly well for a problem-solving new invention.

Use the PAS technique in conjunction with the whole sales process. Qualify your potential customer by establishing their needs. Establish if they are the decision-maker and what their needs and desires are. Ask them questions: 'What's the most important thing to you about ...?' 'What's the main thing you need your ... whatever, to be able to do?' Listen to their answers and assign value to the importance of their needs; establish where you are in the process. Constantly check where your customer is in relation to their proximity to making a decision – ask pre-closing questions, things like: 'No need for a colander and less washing up – how does that sound to you?' Or 'The safety features are important – especially if you are teaching children. Don't you agree?' Make a connection with them; find communalities and a level of easy communication. Try matching and mirroring their behaviour and body language; follow the patterns and pauses of their voice and speak to them in their language.

Understanding your customer will help you deliver a winning solution. You know what is important to them and therefore will find it easy to capture their attention by explaining the problem to them in terms that they can relate to and will understand. This is where the PAS technique is useful.

Re-iterate their problem, agitate it to be sure that they have established an emotional connection with it and then quite calmly, eloquently and assertively present them with their solution. Once you're confident that they are ready to buy, simply ask for the close. Keep quiet and wait for their answer.

As your confidence grows, you will soon start to really enjoy the process of selling to your customers. As they begin to thank you more and more,

❝ the art of selling really is as fun and rewarding as the art of creating ❞

collect these testimonials and ask for referrals and watch as your customer base magnetically grows.

The art of selling really is as fun and rewarding as the art of creating; it's just a question of understanding how. Enjoy the positive results!

---

signposts to success

- If you think that you need to **support your sales process** more by marketing your ideas and business – turn to page 127.
- If you decide that you are ready to **publicly disclose your ideas** – turn to page 47.
- If your best option is going to be to **plan your business better** – turn to page 55.
- If you need to **raise funding** in order to proceed – turn to page 70.

How to attract more of 'the right' attention by marketing and promoting your business

Sales support

As soon as you have secured your intellectual property and developed a product to sell, whether this be the IP itself or manufactured goods and services, you are going to need to start marketing your innovation against the fierce competition of your industry.

If the image of a massive marketing campaign that's going to cost the earth appears before your eyes – fear not. This has got nothing to do with big marketing budgets. In fact, it's got nothing to do with budgets at all. Budgets, in my opinion, are there to restrict your capabilities. They set rules and limitations beyond which you have no means to go. They seek to set boundaries on uncharted terrain and they have no place in the world of invention.

Return on investment

66 consider and measure everything you spend developing your brainwaves on the basis of the return it brings in 99

Rather than focusing on budgets, what we want to talk about is the **return on your investment**. After all, isn't what we are doing building up something to have greater value in the future? In bringing an invention to market you have been making an investment in your future. Now you want to start making a return.

From now on, I would like you to consider and measure everything you spend in relation to developing your brainwaves on the basis of the return it brings in – the return on your investment (ROI). Your marketing should be treated in exactly this way.

If you were to spend £100 on your marketing and that £100 investment made you £300 in return would you be prepared to invest more money? I should think so. Imagine if, every time you went to a betting shop and placed a £10 bet, you were guaranteed to get £30 back – you'd be down there every day. Worse than that, you'd soon be placing bets of £100 – even £1,000 or more. Who knows how much money you would be prepared to spend? Perhaps millions? Definitely millions … if every time you placed your bet you were *guaranteed* to get three times as much in return.

This is what we want to achieve with your marketing. But, it all starts with an initial £10 bet. You need to start out small, with small market tests. You need to trial out different methods so that you can find out what works best for you and your business and you want to test and measure everything that you do. Sounds complicated? I think you're going to find this part fun!

As a rule of thumb, people tend to buy from you only after they have had at least 7 points of contact with you or your business. Another rule of thumb is that the average person only acknowledges 1 in 3 pieces of advertising he or she sees. I'm sure you don't find these rules surprising, but you need to be aware of them when you consider how to deliver your message to your audience.

If people are only going to buy from you after they've crossed paths with you 7 times and there is a strong likelihood that they are going to ignore 2 out of 3 attempts you make to grab their attention, then why not increase your chances and try to attract them in 21 different ways?

But before we look at that, we need to clarify a little bit more marketing terminology.

Identify your market

Let's talk about people

Target market   Marketing managers talk about target market in terms of numbers and letters: 'Oh yes, we're targeting AB1s and ignoring the B2s and Cs', or 'This is aimed at the A1 affluent market', 'No, much more mass-market – ABC1 perhaps?' The truth is that this means nothing to most of us and not a huge amount more to most who use the terminology. So, please don't be tempted by this jargon.

> ❝ narrowing your target market down to a specific group of like-minded individuals is the only way to send a clear and focused message their way ❞

Your target market is a group of people who you are targeting your product towards. In all instances, certain types of people are likely to respond a lot more quickly than others to your new invention. It is important to identify who these people are, target them specifically and then find more of them.

Qualified sales leads These are the people you want to attract. You want to collect their contact details and begin a relationship with them. A well-qualified lead is someone who you have identified as being a very close match to the most responsive category in your target market. It is someone who has expressed interest in having a relationship with you and your company and who is in the position to make a positive purchasing decision.

Take my example of the saucepan, for instance. Almost every household in the country has a saucepan so, in theory, that is the potential size of my target market. However, it is unlikely that, right at this minute, every household in the country is thinking that they need to own an innovative, new, ergonomic pan. Therefore, I need to be more specific and identify who responds to my product first. The people who respond the fastest are those who are going to benefit from this design the most.

In the case of Doctor Cook, the people who benefit the most from the design of the ergonomic handle are people who are suffering from weak or painful wrists. The product has been designed to make cooking easier for everybody, but these individuals notice the benefits first. They suffer from the pain and strain of lifting a hot, heavy saucepan and the Doctor Cook design is an obvious solution. These individuals are my **primary focus target market**.

Women are 5 times more likely to cook than men and 3 times more likely to suffer from a strain-related injury so I can narrow my target market down further – and further still by taking into account that, by the age of 65, 50% of us are likely to be suffering from arthritis. If I then identify someone who is in this category *and* in the process of buying a new cooker, I know I have found a really 'hot' or very well-qualified lead.

It is important that you identify early on who the early adopters or primary focused target markets in your business are. Once you have met a few of them, start to try to stereotype them. Get to know them and understand what drives them. Learn how to speak their language. Then start to find more people in similar situations.

An ex-colleague of mine, the then marketing manager, taught me the concept of **profiling your target market**. She had developed names for her market sectors and portrayed them as rounded characters. As a team, we grew quite fond of them as we really started to understand them. Doris, Audrey and Zoe, we called them. We'd even detailed down to where they went on their summer holidays and what sort of souvenirs they'd be bringing back: Doris the Costa del Sol ashtray, Audrey, some local pottery or a pot of honey and Zoe, the scuba diving instructor's phone number ...

Visualise the people and individuals your product is aimed at. Give them names and really start to understand their characters. This will help you deliver your message in a way to which they will respond.

❝ work out who exactly your primary focus target market is and look to attract more people who are the same ❞

Work out who exactly your primary focus target market is and look to attract more people who are the same. The better you get to know these people as individuals, the better equipped you will be to deliver to them exactly what they need as they need it – **these are the fundamentals of great marketing.**

Develop a positive relationship

Once you have been invited by an individual to use his or her contact details, use these responsibly and amicably. Build a positive relationship by offering advice, information and entertainment that they will enjoy and respond well to. Do not be tempted to be too pushy for the sale. Your aim is to become a **'welcome guest'** in their homes and not an **'annoying pest'**. Consider how you would like to be approached and what information you would like to receive if you were them. Present yourself as a warm authority on your subject. You are someone who your target market can trust to provide helpful and useful services right when they are needed most. You are both their leader and their guide in respect of your area of expertise and you should seek to position yourself as such.

❝ great marketing is all about developing a lasting (and profitable) relationship with your target market ❞

Great marketing is all about developing a lasting (and profitable) relationship with your target market. It is about adopting a multi-media, multi-market approach to delivering your message in a focused, informative and fun way. It's about testing it out on a small scale with a few people until you have a positive response. Then, as you grow in confidence, in line with more positive results, you can start to build up the investment you make and the consequent return.

Top 21 attention-grabbers

1. Knowing people's names

People always respond well if you use their name. Try to use people's names as often as possible. Even if you are sending out a generic broadcast or mailing it can be worthwhile personalising each mail-out. If you are using email, then a decent auto responder should make this simple to set up. The more personal a relationship you can build with your customers and sales leads the more rewarding it will be.

2. Focused message

Deliver a personal and focused message appropriate to the person who is receiving it. Remember: Most people only really absorb **one key message at a time**. Do not try to deliver too much information in one go. Keep your message clear, focused and specific to the reader.

3. Strong headline

Always use a strong headline. This is what grabs people's attention and makes them sit up and listen to what you have to say. Skim through any newspaper and see what catches your attention and why.

The sole purpose of a headline is to grab people's attention and encourage them to find out more. Use a headline with as much of your marketing material as you can. Use it at the top of a sales letter or the start of a presentation; print it on the front of a leaflet and on your packaging – **grab people's attention** by stating clearly and boldly why they need to know about you. Test out different headlines and work out which ones produce the best response.

4. Unique selling points

Stimulate people's desires by portraying your unique selling points (USPs) as clearly defined, interesting and unique benefits to the end user. Your USPs are, in effect, your competitive edge. Be clear about what this is and make sure you show it off.

5. Offers and promotions

AIDA

AIDA stands for Attention, Interest, Desire and Action. It is also my favourite opera, so an easy one to remember.

Whenever you are laying out any sales or marketing material consider the AIDA formula. Grab people's attention with a strong headline. Stimulate their interests and desires in the 'meat' of your material and finish with a strong call to ACTION.

Visit our website www.FromBrainwaveToBusiness.com for further details.

Offers and promotions can be a great way to grab people's attention or encourage them to make a repeat purchase. Supermarkets and large chain stores use offers and promotions all the time. Consider whether you can tie an offer in to a public holiday or leap-frog on the back of a successful event.

Think inspiringly about your offers and promotions. People are bombarded by such things every day. What is going to make yours stand out in a crowd?

Offers and promotions work very well when presented to people with who you have an existing relationship. Build solid relationships and present irresistible offers.

Offers that work:

- free (something)
- one free for every three you buy
- two for 20% less
- buy one, get one free.

Using a **money-back guarantee** is a fantastic way to remove any perceived risk that the buyer might have in terms of investing in your offer. Doing so might even boost your sales. Test it and see.

6. Competitions

Running a free-entry competition can be a very useful tool to collect new leads for your business. Make it exciting, interesting and relevant to the services you offer. Be sure to announce the winner!

7. Free giveaways

Free giveaways are another way to attract people to your business. Start your relationship with a new lead by giving something away free. You can either tie in with another business and promote this as a joint venture or simply offer a free report to anyone interested in your area of expertise. You can then begin to develop a relationship with these individuals and hopefully convert them to valuable, returning customers.

8. Media

When considering your marketing you need to think in terms of a multi-media approach. Technology and the ability to communicate have become so dynamic and easily accessible that you need to take advantage of as many different types of media as you can to deliver your message. Here are some of your options:

- direct mail
- email

> **when considering your marketing you need to think in terms of a multi-media approach**

- telephone
- fax (this works simply because nobody else is doing it anymore)
- text message
- voice broadcast
- video
- online.

Approaching your customers using more than one method of communication can be a great way to strengthen your relationship with them. Build this into your marketing campaign.

9. Online

In today's electronic age, you need a presence online. Think about how a website or blog could best work to help you market your business. Remember, exactly the same principles apply online as they do anywhere else in marketing. Decide what you want your customers to do when they reach your website, ask them to do this and make it as easy as possible for them to achieve.

Online, you have the ability to attract the attention of a massive worldwide audience. Going after everybody is going to get you nowhere. Be very specific about the people you wish to attract. Collect their contact details and start building a relationship. Online, more than ever, you will need to gain people's trust before they start spending their hard-earned money with you.

10. TV, radio and printed press

Television channels, magazines, newspapers, local and national radio stations are always looking for great stories. Attracting their attention by sending out a well-structured press release can be an excellent way to get some high-quality coverage of you and your business.

Build relationships with journalists and the media just as you would with your customers. Keep them up-to-date with your latest news and let them know how to contact you. You can always ask a specific editor or producer to provide you with the show schedule or events calendar. In this way, you can approach them with an angle which is both of interest and relevant to other features they are covering simultaneously.

Once you have appeared in the media, you can use this coverage to add credibility to your business and reputation.

11. Press release

Being able to write a fantastic press release and grab the media's attention is a really useful tool to have at your disposal. PR media coverage attracts leads to your business, adds to your credibility and raises your overall profile.

Use a press release to convey your initial message. Be prepared with a list of questions that you would like the presenter or interviewer to ask you and have an up-to-date biography and photograph ready in case they ask. Do not be tempted to look for a 'hook' to your story. Hooks are for

How to grab attention

ATTN: Name the recipient

For immediate release (state the release date)

USE A STRONG HEADLINE TO ATTRACT PEOPLE'S ATTENTION

Next you need to retain their attention by disclosing an overall summary which includes the juicy bits in your story and why these will be of benefit, interest and entertainment to their audience.

Then use bullet points:

- to retain interest and stimulate desire
- to disclose fascinating facts and figures
- to draw their attention to the benefits of you being on their TV show or writing an article about you.

Ensure the whole content is valuable to the reader. They should benefit and be inspired by your messages. Make the message about them and not you.

> **Isolate your key message or objective. If you are presenting a special offer or need to draw attention to one specific attraction then isolate this from the rest of the text.**

A simple form works best. Use a plain font and do not be tempted to baffle the recipient with too much information. Keep it to one page and leave them wanting to know more ...

Describe yourself succinctly, explaining why you would interest and benefit their audience.

Be sure to give a clear call to action.

Give clear details as to how they should contact you.

hanging coats on. You want to be delivering information, helpful advice and news which will interest or entertain the receiver. Think about your target market (in this instance, the viewers, listeners or readers exposed to your release) and how your message will best interest them and deliver this in your press release. Reveal yourself and your character, make it interesting and fascinating, provide facts and information which you are able to qualify upon request and be prepared to talk about your story.

12. Networking

This is a great way to generate new business leads and industry contacts – start getting involved with events and gatherings that take place in your community, in your industry, both on- and off-line. Join an inventor network, a business network and a social network – the better linked in you are the more accessible you are to your target market.

13 Forums and blogging

The internet gives you and your business the opportunity to reach millions and millions of people at the click of a button. Forums and blogging can be a great way to start achieving this. A search online is bound to reveal a forum or blog where your target market hangs out. Join and become a member.

Remember though, you are not on there to sell; you are there to share in this community. You have lots of useful information and knowledge which will be of value to the other members; share this with them and build up a relationship. When you have established yourself as someone who can be trusted, you will be welcomed as being really helpful when you offer some product recommendation.

Do not be tempted to disguise who you really are or to make up exaggerated stories about yourself and your business. You will soon get caught out. By all means use a pseudonym or an avatar to represent you, just remember that these online bloggers are quick to spot a fraud – the last thing you need is to be refused access.

Forums and blogging can be great fun. They can also be a good way to acquire some really useful knowledge yourself. Experiment – but be warned. It can become addictive. Do not be tempted to waste too much time!

Places to test (among countless others):

- Alibaba – great if you are promoting manufactured goods or services
- Bebo – social and general network
- CafeMom – great if you are promoting mother and child products
- Facebook – social network (join the Brainwave to Business group)
- Google blogger – free blogging from Google
- LinkedIn – fantastic for building business-to-business relationships (join the Brainwave to Business group)
- LiveJournal – online blogging
- Myspace – general personal blog site

- Orkut – social networking site owned by Google and popular in Asia & S. America
- Tagged – general network with over 70 million users
- Twitter – real-time short messaging service
- Windows Live Spaces – blogging, formally MSN services

14. Trusted leader

It is your job to become the trusted leader in your business and market. This role escalates in line with the relationships you build with your customers, within your industry and in the wider community.

Celebrities sell products, this is a known fact. Develop yourself as a celebrity within your industry. 'Warm and authoritative' is the role you need to play. You know more about your subject than anyone else – you are, after all, the inventor, creator or founder of your business and you should position yourself in line with the respect you deserve.

15. Endorsements and testimonials

What other people say about your business, products or services can be infinitely more valuable than the bold statements you make yourself. Next time somebody pays you a compliment ask if they would mind if you wrote it down and used it in your marketing material.

Get into the habit of collecting testimonials from customers who have been delighted by your services. Use these whenever you can. I often print testimonials on the back of my letterhead and always try to include as many as possible in any leaflet or printed material we prepare.

It can be a good idea to make a point of collecting some celebrity endorsements or testimonials. The more credibility you can build behind the unique selling points you are offering the easier it will become to position yourself as a warm and trusted authority in the market.

16. Direct mail and voice mail

Send stuff to people or get in touch by phone. Make it interesting and personal. People love to receive letters through the mail from a friend or family member – it's the junk that drives them insane. Think about being a 'welcome guest' and not an 'annoying pest' and develop some interesting ways of attracting and engaging your customer's attention, either by mail or voice mail.

Leaving a voice mail on someone's answering machine letting them know that you were thinking about them and asking how they are getting on with your new invention can be a welcome and unexpected surprise to a customer who may well buy from you again. Equally, writing to somebody after they have purchased your product to enquire how they are finding using it and offering them some helpful advice in the meantime can be a great way to build customer loyalty and grow recurring sales.

> 66 start with an attention-grabbing headline and end with a clear call to action 99

As with all of your marketing material, the more interesting and personal to the receiver's needs your correspondence can be, the more positive the results you will be likely to see. Start with an attention-grabbing headline and end with a clear call to action. Test on a small scale and work to constantly improve your results.

17. Advertising and pay per click

Advertising both online and offline can be an immensely rewarding way to generate new business. It can also cost a small fortune and bring in absolutely no revenue at all.

Consider who you want to appeal to, what message you want to deliver and how you want your audience to respond before you start spending lots of money. Pay per click can be an affordable way to test out headlines and marketing messages. Once you have got it working online you can begin to experiment on a small scale offline. Be aware of the fact that most big companies tend to cut their marketing budgets in times of recession. This means that advertising sales are struggling so you may well be able to negotiate yourself a bargain.

Unless you are Coca-Cola, Nike, Virgin or similar, do not be tempted to brand advertise. Nobody knows who you are, and in this instance, they simply don't care. Advertise with a message that will appeal to them instead, or try offering them something free in exchange for their contact details. In this way, you can use your initial advert to generate leads you can later convert into sales.

Test and measure and grow accordingly.

18. Exhibitions and public events

Attending exhibitions and events which specifically attract your target market is a fabulous way to see lots of well-qualified leads all in the right mindset to place orders. The downside of attending such events is that you are competing alongside everybody else who is also trying to get access to the same target market.

You are going to need to work hard on your presentation so that your exhibition stand, stands out. Think of some innovative ways to capture people's contact details – run a competition, for instance, and make sure you ask everyone you speak to to leave their business card behind. Start building long-term relationships that you can later convert into profitable sales.

19. Public speaking and seminars

If you've got the confidence and the capability then you have definitely got a story to tell and doing so from a public platform positions you as a trusted leader and warm authority. Public speaking and the hosting of seminars can be a really productive way to generate more leads for your business and increase your profile in the process. As with everything, start small and build up as you gain confidence and have a successful track record.

It is certainly worth testing this, and getting over your stage fright. The more public speaking you do, the more comfortable it will become and, as your business grows, you can expect to be asked to do more and more. It can be a good idea to start getting comfortable with it now.

20. Publishing

Publishing a book or e-book can be a great way to grab people's attention. It also adds credibility to you as the author and helps to tell the story behind your innovation. Are you surprised that most of my examples mention Doctor Cook?

21. Clear call to action

Always tell people what you would like them to do next.

There is a reason why your call to action is delivered in your closing statement. The last thing you say is likely to be the thing most remembered. Tell people clearly what action you would like them to take. Give them more than one option by which to respond. If you are inviting them to contact you then make it as easy as possible for them to do so. Provide a telephone number and email address, a website, a postal address, fax number, etc.

If you are inviting people to purchase from you then, again, make it easy for them to do so by offering more than one option. Can they buy online, with a credit card, by mail-order or over the telephone? Offer as many options as possible to broaden your opportunities. By testing and measuring the response rate to different approaches you will soon gauge how your target market responds best.

PR and marketing agents

Don't be tempted to delegate too much of your marketing – not until you have fully understood it all anyway. How you market your business basically boils down to **how you buy sales**. If you are asking somebody else to 'buy sales' on your behalf it is less easy to be sure of the results and to monitor the return on your investment. You need this sort of information to make progress.

❝ how you market your business basically boils down to how you buy sales ❞

Just as I would advise never delegating the cheque book to anyone else in your business, I also recommend that you keep hold of the marketing. Both more or less equate to the same thing.

So, to summarise: use a **clear and focused message** delivered via a **multi-media approach** to match the needs of a **defined target market**. First **test on a small scale** and respond by growing in line with positive results to obtain **a healthy return on your investment**.

signposts to success

- If you decide you need to **brush up your sales skills** – turn to page 101.

- If you want to find out more about how **to test and measure your marketing** – turn to page 127.

- If you feel like you're ready to **disclose your invention publicly** – turn to page 47.

- If you want some more **ideas about what to do next** – turn to page 26.

- If you would like to join the Brainwave to Business groups on LinkedIn or Facebook join our forum discussions and benefit from brainstorming in a community with likeminded individuals. Visit www.FromBrainwaveToBusiness.com for the details.

12

How to test, measure and continually optimise everything you do

The development cycle

If you have read the section on developing your ideas further or if you've familiarised yourself with the process of business planning then you will have understood that nothing is ever perfect first time. This chapter deals with the process of striving for perfection by constantly and continually testing, measuring and optimising everything you do.

Development of anything, whether it is your ideas, your business plans, your marketing material or your overall business strategy, happens in stages. First you generate ideas, then you test them. Next you measure these results and finally you consider what actions can be taken to optimise this development before going back to the drawing board and starting the whole process again. If you can understand and identify these development cycles, you will become able to work your way through them more and more quickly. You'll be better able to monitor your progress and you'll find taking action easier and more productive. Doing so will save you a lot of time and anxiety. It will also save you a considerable amount of money. For this reason, it is worth your while becoming disciplined in your approach to testing and monitoring your progress.

Darwin first noticed that evolution in nature happened in cycles, but it's not just in nature that such principles apply. When you begin a new project or activity, you start with an initial idea. Your starting point becomes the outer perimeter of the first development cycle, albeit at a point that is relatively far away from where you intend to go. This initial cycle has a comparatively large radius and you will find that progress in the early days appears slow. This is because you are pushing forward, uncovering new terrain, breaking down boundaries and evolving the outline structure of your creation. As you move through the cycles, the territory you are covering will become more familiar to you. You will get that sense of having been in this place before – except that you're not. You're one revolution closer; you've got one cycle of progress against which you can compare your results. You might feel as though you are back at the beginning but you're really getting closer to your end goal: perfection. As you get closer and closer, the momentum will start to build. You will feel as though the cycles are spinning faster; your results will become more precise and the force of your actions stronger and more efficient.

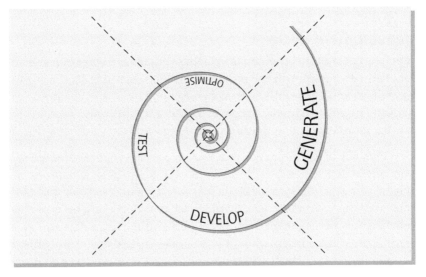

A Zen master was once overheard saying that 'a spinning top appears motionless when it's spinning fastest'. This is ultimately what we are all striving for in our businesses: the point at which the action and energy required to motivate and drive our business appear easy and effortless. At this point, you have effectively reached the centre of the development cycle; you are in the eye of the storm, so to speak, and there is a sense of calm and tranquillity that efficiently carries your success forward. It is as close to perfection as you could possibly come and this is what we strive for in our development.

Testing and measuring

Testing: A procedure for critical evaluation; a means of determining the presence, quality, or truth of something; a trial

Measuring: Ascertaining the dimensions, quantity, or capacity by comparison with a standard norm

Optimising: Making as perfect or effective as possible

Your challenge is to create systems for testing and measuring your activities from which you can draw meaningful and comparative results that will aid and enhance your progress.

Throughout this book the importance of not expecting to achieve for perfection first time has been reiterated. Development of any kind requires a degree of failure as it is only by making such mistakes that we are ever likely to learn. Many of the most successful people in the world are also those who have experienced the greatest amount of failure. Take Richard Branson, for instance – whether in his attempts to fly around the world in a hot air balloon, his bid to buy the national lottery or his efforts to dominate the high street with cosmetic counters, he has failed repeatedly. Rather than be dissuaded by such negative outcomes, Branson merely embraces this as a series of results from which he can learn, improve and make progress. It is with this constructive mindset that you should approach the task of testing and measuring.

❝ development of any kind requires a degree of failure as it is only by making such mistakes that we are ever likely to learn ❞

1 What activities are you currently involved in?
2 Do you know which activities are working best for you?
3 If not, what can you do to find out?
4 How could you systemise your testing and measuring?
5 What specifically are you able to test and measure?
6 Who is going to record this information and how?
7 What can you learn from these results?

These are questions that you need to ask yourself continually. Test and measure everything you do and look to improve your results as you monitor your progress. If you don't do this then you are literally relying on fate and luck to carry you forward. Flinging enough mud at the wall in the hope that some of it might stick can be a huge waste of energy. If 50% of what you are doing is working, what about the 50% that is not? This is simply a waste of half your time and resources. Better to know for certain and learn from your mistakes than allow them to catch up with you and cost you a small fortune.

Make it work before you make it big

Start testing on a small scale first. This is one of the fundamental principles of testing and optimising. If it goes wrong, it really doesn't matter. You can afford to lose that old cereal packet by turning it into your first prototype, for example. You can afford to lose 50 sheets of A4 paper cut into 4 and posted through 200 letterboxes in your neighbourhood. You can also afford to lose an afternoon testing out your sales pitch on a local market stall. But, can you afford to lose that one big buyer? Can you afford to lose the cost of the wrong mass-production tools? Can you afford to put your house behind an idea and then for it all to go horribly wrong?

You should not be prepared to take such risks. No right-minded investor would consider such serious exposure and neither should you. Make it work for you on a small scale and, once you've tested, measured and improved something to the best of your ability, only then should you start to gradually scale it up. If it works with 5 people, roll it out to 50 people; if it works with 50 people, then try it on 250; then 500, 1,000, 5,000 and so on ... Make sure that you are going to get the positive results you anticipate before you start growing and grow at a speed that you can afford.

Test and measure systematically

Decide on the process of testing and measuring an activity before you begin. Set a benchmark or precedent against which you can compare your results. Use spreadsheets and result logs to keep records of the measurements you take and assess the scale upon which such results are being judged.

Systematic measuring is about establishing an organised discipline under which you can scrutinise the performance of your actions unambiguously and without being affected by emotional or instinctive opinions. It is about proving your ideas, not just to yourself but to your team, potential investors and, ultimately, the market you are trying to sell into.

What to test and measure

"everything you do will benefit from being tested and measured"

In theory, everything you do will benefit from being tested and measured. Different activities require different types of testing. The important issue is to establish a protocol for extracting tangible and comparative results which you can analyse and use to improve the performance of the activities you do.

Here is a list of elements you could be testing, measuring and optimising:

- your brainwaves
- your prototypes
- your products and services
- your sales order fulfilment
- your channels of distribution
- your customer service
- your advertising
- your pay per click campaign
- your press releases
- your public relations
- your sales pitch
- your sales letters
- your elevator pitch
- your website
- your website visitor conversion rates (the rates at which visitors become customers)
- your lead conversion rates

... and so the list goes on.

Think about the concept of testing and measuring in relation to your marketing. Say you spent £10 printing a flyer on your own printer that, when distributed in your local neighbourhood – perhaps to 200 houses – generated 5 leads, which over a period of time, became loyal customers worth £100 each to your business. It would then be worth your while investing £100 to have 2,000 leaflets printed, knowing that you can expect approximately 50 new customers as a result.

Split testing

You might like to consider split testing. In other words, rather than simply distributing 200 leaflets, generating 5 positive results and deciding to upscale immediately, you choose to test and optimise first. Say you created 4 different leaflets by testing different headlines, or different graphics, different colours or different marketing messages and, whereas one leaflet generated 5 positive results, another generated 8 or even 10. You would know that this second leaflet performed better than the first one and, consequently, this would be the one you would choose to produce and distribute in great volumes.

When you are doing a split test such as the one mentioned above, it is important to test only one change at a time. For instance, send out exactly the same leaflet with 4 different headlines or printed on 4 different colours of paper. Only in this way can you be certain which colour or which headline performs better than the others as changing too much at once will leave you unsure as to why your results have improved or got worse.

❝ there is very rarely only one way to do anything. What you need is proof that one idea works better than another ❞

This same concept applies to developing your ideas. Don't be too blinkered or fixed on one particular solution. Sure, it might work, but can it work better? There is very rarely only one way to do anything. What you need is proof that one idea works better than another and it should be on this basis that all your decisions are made. Test everything. All of the data you gather will be worth its weight in gold as your business grows.

Choose the right measure

You can be as creative and different as you like when choosing which measure will best apply to a specific activity. The results are for your purpose and, so long as you and your team understand them, there is no reason why you need to stick to predefined standards. Your measurements need to be tangible and quantifiable. You need to be able to use them to measure, improve and acccelerate your progress. It might be that you are looking for a simple Yes/No answer or that you are extracting complex or multi-dimensional numerical data. Either way, it is important that you choose units of measure that are appropriate to your methods of testing and that you maintain these as a standard throughout the development process.

The more data you collect, the more accurate your results will become. Asking 5 people will give you some indication of your potential for success in the market. Asking 500 people will give you a much more conclusive result. Use these results to support your decision-making process and make improvements in your actions accordingly.

Use your results

You would be amazed by how many people take the time to test and measure but then fail to use these results to make improvements to the systems, products, services and activities that they have been testing. SAT tests in schools have been used to test the performance of the education system and yet so many resources have been poured into testing and measuring results that little is left for improvements. Avoid making this same mistake.

It is important to test and measure but it is more important to use your results to implement positive changes, to improve and make progress.

The 80:20 principle

You can analyse your results on the basis of the Pareto principle. This principle is also known as the 80:20 rule and states that, in many situations, 80% of the effects come from 20% of the cause. In all likelihood, 80% of your revenue will be generated by 20% of your customers. Therefore, what would happen to your revenue if you were to concentrate on attracting more customers like your top 20%?

You can apply the 80:20 rule to many aspects of your business (and personal life). Probably you wear 20% of your clothes 80% of the time; you invest 80% of your resources on 20% of your actions; you spend 80% of your time dealing with 20% of your problems. Think about how you can improve efficiency with this knowledge. If you could spend 20% of your time dealing with 80% of your problems, how much better would your life (and business) become?

Find out what's working and do more of it!

It is through constant testing and measuring that your results and performance will improve. It is by being aware of the 80% that isn't

ᒪᒪ become a master of measurement and remember to apply your results ꟻꟻ

working that you can start to align your actions with your anticipated outcomes to make a real and positive difference in the performance, efficiency and profitability of your business. This is why testing, measuring and continually striving for perfection is fundamentally what all successful businesses do.

Become a master of measurement and remember to apply your results.

signposts to success

- If you decide that you are ready to start developing your invention by testing and evaluating your results – turn to page 26.

- If you now wish to consider how best you could optimise your sales strategy – turn to page 101.

- If you like the principles of magnetic attraction and see this as a good way to drive customers to your business, then find out just how you can attract the right attention – turn to page 112.

What to do if somebody has stolen your idea

Proof of ownership, evidence of theft

Scream a bit, shout and cry, jump up and down, punch a brick wall (but don't break your hand because you are going to need this very shortly) ... and then **calm yourself right down**. You need to be thinking as clearly and with as much focus as you possibly can and any emotions you are harbouring are going to impede you from doing so. **You'll have to take some fast action.**

What you need to accumulate are facts and evidence. You need proof that your idea has been stolen and for this, you have to be sure that the idea is yours in the first place.

Is the idea definitely yours?

Registering your intellectual property rights provides you with exclusive rights over your ideas. If you have secured your official intellectual property rights (patents, design registrations and trade marks) then, enforcing them is straightforward. If you are enforcing your rights over unregistered IP such as copyrights and designs you will need to be able to provide evidence to justify your claims.

> **❝ the more evidence you can gather of somebody infringing your IP, the stronger your case against them will be ❞**

The need for proof

The more evidence you can gather of somebody infringing your IP, the stronger your case against them will be. Amass as much information as possible and then contact the law-enforcement authorities (the police, Revenue and Customs and Trading Standards) and your trusted businesses partners.

If you suspect that your IP is being infringed, you should always consider reporting this to the law-enforcement authorities, even if it is only a minor case of infringement. It is impossible for them to provide total security all of the time and information that you provide may give missing details or a new angle on an investigation into organised crime. Crime figures for IP infringement and the trading of counterfeit goods are on the rise. It is important that you take action against criminals. The more people taking action, the more the criminals will be dissuaded from copying or stealing IP.

As soon as you contact the law-enforcement authorities they will want to know details of your case. Work with them to provide this information. The more information you can provide, the faster and easier it will be for the authorities to respond.

You should expect to provide:

- a description of the goods that is detailed enough for the authorities to identify them or information that identifies the consignment or packages
- information on the type of infringement – whether your rights are covered by a patent, or trade mark
- proof that you hold the relevant rights
- confirmation of whether you hold the rights yourself or are acting as the authorised representative or agent of the right-holder
- the name and address of a contact person.

Where possible, you should also include:

- the location and intended destination of the goods
- when the goods are expected to arrive or depart
- the identity of the importer or exporter
- the country of production
- the transport routes being used.

Keep detailed records, including an example of the counterfeit product, for yourself, and provide the authorities and your trusted business partners with all details as well. Add to these as they arise.

Preparing your case

Should your case end up in court, be prepared to contribute to preparing your legal case and take an active role in the investigation. You will be acting as a witness and, in doing so, you will be helping the case for the prosecution. The more evidence you can provide, the stronger your case will be.

Points you need to prepare:

- your status and your authority to act as an expert witness
- your examination of the counterfeit goods and statement accordingly
- proof that an offence has been committed
- proof of your IP rights (registered certificate)
- confirmation that you have not granted permission to use your rights to the person accused
- a statement of events in chronological order
- a statement about how securely the above evidence has been stored.

If you do act as an expert witness then be aware that you may be asked to appear in court. In the event that this happens, prepare well in advance, remain calm on the day and answer all questions as accurately and informatively as you can. Oh, and wear blue ... apparently it's the colour of innocence!

❝ take precautionary measures to avoid infringement ❞

Precautionary measures

To avoid being in the situation of having to defend your IP it is a good idea to take as many precautionary measures as possible to avoid infringement in the first place.

1. Intellectual property

Register your IP and keep the rights to your IP up-to-date and well guarded. Maintain records of your development process and build evidence chronologically as it occurs.

2. Packaging and product design

Design your products and their packaging so that these are as difficult to copy as possible. Holograms and other such labelling can be a good way to achieve this. Use unique technologies and 'secret' materials which you develop specifically to deter counterfeit versions. **Remember:** counterfeit goods always look cheap and nasty. Avoid this look in your original design.

Take steps to:

- Match the product, serial codes, model numbers and further details across the packaging. Fake versions will be easier to spot if the numbers don't match.
- Give your contact details. Illegitimate operations will often avoid doing so.
- Include a guarantee or safety certificate.
- Use your logo and graphic style on your packaging and keep this consistent across your range.
- Include barcodes, trade marks, patent information and recycling instructions, making it harder to copy.
- Make sure there are no spelling mistakes – these are common in counterfeit goods.

3. Manufacture and supply

Build trusted relationships with reputable outsourced suppliers. Do your research and only employ reputable and authorised suppliers. Check out their references. Use business information agencies and Companies House records to find out as much background information as you can. Taking the time to make the right decision about which manufacturer to use will ultimately save you time and money.

Make sure that genuine material is being used in the production of your goods. Inspect this material and inspect the production process. Develop guidance for manufacturers and suppliers and make sure that they follow this. Ask for invoices and keep them. Make sure that your goods are delivered in sealed, secure and tamper-proof packaging and maintain these standards.

4. Channels of distribution

It is not just your suppliers that you should be checking before you do business with them. Run background checks on your customers too. Set systems so that sales and marketing teams can be sure that customers are legitimate and have legitimate outlets for selling or distributing your goods.

Monitoring customer buying patterns and making further checks when you notice anything out of the ordinary can be a good way to prevent a problem occurring. It can be a sensible idea to develop a guidance manual, giving wholesalers and customers clear advice on what you expect from them. A legally binding contract or written agreement should always take into consideration how disputes between you will be resolved.

IP is a risky business. The lure of huge rewards makes it prey to criminals and corporations looking to take their share of the action. For this reason it is often the subject of disagreements between businesses, individuals and organisations. The main issues invariably relate to money and the control of the IP. It is important always to think about how your rights may be used.

5. Run system checks

Keep your eyes and ears open. If necessary, employ scouts and 'mystery shoppers' to search the market on your behalf. Measure the amount of material that is being used by your suppliers, run regular internet searches and visit industry events. Check your systems regularly so as to spot the possibility of counterfeits.

6. Waste disposal

Make sure that your waste is disposed of and recycled securely. Be extra cautious about how you dispose of or destroy confidential material.

7. Build awareness

Not everybody is as clued up about IP as you are. Educate your team, colleagues, suppliers and customers about intellectual property. If you make them aware of these issues, they will also be on the lookout for potential infringers and if you do need to react, well-prepared procedures will make it easy for you to do so fast and efficiently.

❝ as ridiculous as this may sound, someone infringing your IP should be seen as flattery to your amazing design ❞

To have somebody infringing your IP can be frustrating, infuriating, heartbreaking and demoralising. **It is in reality a massive compliment.** As ridiculous as this may sound, someone infringing your IP should be seen as flattery to your amazing design. What's not good is if they are making a lot of money from it and you are not.

Defend what is right. Just avoid getting too bogged down in the detail. You've got a head full of ideas and loads of positive energy. Do not let the pirates ruin your health. Stay true to what you know is right but be cautious of the risks and honest with yourself. Sometimes it's best to let go ... at other times you have to stand firm and say No!

Take as many precautions as possible to avoid the situation in the first place. Join anti-copying membership schemes and look out for initiatives to prevent copying in your industry or geographical areas. Having access to these sorts of resources can be hugely beneficial should the need for support arise.

Seek as much expert legal advice as you can afford and speak to people who have been in your situation. Build relationships with lawyers and IP attorneys in advance so that if the situation arises you are ready to act fast. Start saving a pot of emergency funds that allow you to react rapidly if you need to.

Good luck and keep going!

---

signposts to success

- For a quick glance at the **law of England and Wales** with regard to intellectual property theft – see opposite where a few extracts have been assembled for your reference.

- To **test, measure and continually optimise** everything you do – turn to page 127.

- To find out more about how to improve your ability to **protect your IP** by securing it in the first place – turn to page 36.

- To **come up with new ideas** and approach your situation from a different perspective – turn to page 26.

Elements of key offences

Trade Marks Act 1994

Section 92(1) A person commits an offence who with a view to gain for himself or another, or with intent to cause loss to another, and without the consent of the proprietor:

(a) applies to goods or their packaging a sign identical to, or likely to be mistaken for, a registered trade mark, or

(b) sells or lets for hire, offers or exposes for sale or hire or distributes goods which bear, or the packaging of which bears, such a sign, or

(c) has in his possession, custody or control in the course of a business any such goods with a view to the doing of anything, by himself or another, which would be an offence under paragraph b.

Section 92(1) (a), (b), (c), (2) and (3) offences are all hybrid offences, for which a maximum sentence of 10 years' imprisonment and/or an unlimited fine are available by way of penalty on indictment. See Section 92(2) and (3) for other possible offences.

It should be noted that the effect of amendments in the Serious Organised Crime and Police Act 2005 to S24 of the Police and Criminal Evidence Act 1984 means that all these offences are now 'arrestable'. Further guidance can be found in the Police and Criminal Evidence Act (PACE) code G.

Section 92(2) A person commits an offence who with a view to gain for himself or another, or with intent to cause loss to another, and without the consent of the proprietor:

(a) applies a sign identical to, or likely to be taken for, a registered trade mark to material intended to be used –
  i. for labelling or packaging goods,
  ii. as a business paper in relation to goods, or
  iii. for advertising goods, or

(b) uses in the course of a business material bearing such a sign for labelling or packaging goods, as a business paper in relation to goods, or for advertising goods, or

(c) has in his possession, custody or control in the course of a business any such material with a view to the doing of anything, by himself or another, which would be an offence under paragraph (b).

Section 92(3) A person commits an offence who with a view to gain for himself or another, or with intent to cause loss to another, and without the consent of the proprietor.

▶

(a) makes an article specifically designed or adapted for making copies of a sign identical to, or likely to be mistaken for, a registered trade mark, or

(b) has such an article in his possession, custody or control in the course of a business, knowing or having reason to believe that it has been, or is to be, used to produce goods, or material for labelling or packaging goods, as a business paper in relation to goods, or advertising goods.

Copyright, Designs and Patents Act 1988 (CDPA)

Section 107 – Unauthorised copying offences can relate to:

- CDs – music, film, computer software and games
- DVDs – music, film, computer software and games
- Videos – music, film and games
- publications
- books
- photographs and posters.

Section 107(1) A person commits an offence who, without the licence of the copyright owner:

(a) makes for sale or hire, or

(b) imports into the United Kingdom otherwise than for his private and domestic use; or

(c) possesses in the course of a business with a view to committing any act infringing the copyright, or

(d) in the course of a business:

    i.   sells or lets for hire, or

    ii. offers or exposes for sale or hire, or

    iii. exhibits in public, or

    iv. distributes, or

(e) distributes otherwise than in the course of a business to such an extent as to affect prejudicially the owner of the copyright,

an article which is, and which he knows or has reason to believe is, an infringing copy of a copyright work.

Section 107(1) (a), (b), (d) (iv) and (e) above are hybrid offences for which a maximum sentence of 10 years' imprisonment and/or an unlimited fine are available by way of penalty on indictment. Section 107(1) (c), (d) (i), (d) (ii), and (d) (iii) above are purely summary offences for which a maximum sentence of six months and/or a fine of £5,000 are available by way of penalty. See Section 107(2) for other possible offences.

Section 198 Illicit recordings

Section 198 is concerned with illicit recordings (film, music etc). The offences also relate to unauthorised recordings of live performances (sometimes referred to as 'bootlegs'). Bootlegging is the recording, duplication and sale of a performance such as a live concert or broadcast without the permission of the artist or recording company. Section 198 offences are similar to those contained in Section 107 of the Copyright, Designs and Patents Act 1988.

Section 198(1) A person commits an offence who, without the licence of the copyright owner:

(a) makes for sale or hire, or

(b) imports into the United Kingdom otherwise than for his private and domestic use, or

(c) possesses in the course of a business with a view to committing any act infringing the rights conferred by this Part, or

(d) in the course of a business:
    i. sells or lets for hire, or
    ii. offers or exposes for sale or hire, or
    iii. distributes

a recording, which he knows or has reason to believe is an illicit recording.

Section 198(1) (a), (b), (d) and (d) (iii) above are hybrid offences for which a maximum sentence of 10 years' imprisonment and/or an unlimited fine are available by way of penalty on indictment. The other offences under Section 198 carry a mixture of sentences.

Section 296 Copyright protection measures

Section 296 gives protection to technical measures taken by a rights holder to protect copyright works and prevent unauthorised copying. It gives the right to bring proceedings against anyone who deliberately supplies devices, or information which enables or assists the circumvention of technical equipment. In relation to computers and games stations this circumvention is commonly known as 'chipping' and is covered in Section 2962B

In respect of an infringement under Section 296 the copyright owner has the same rights as for offences under Section 107 and 198.

Section 296ZB – Chipping

Section 296ZB(1) A person commits an offence if he:

(a) manufactures for sale or hire, or

(b) imports into the United Kingdom otherwise than for his private and domestic use, or

(c) in the course of a business:
   i.   sells or lets for hire, or
   ii.   offers or exposes for sale or hire, or
   iii. advertises for sale or hire, or
   iv. possesses, or
   v.   distributes, or
   vi. distributes otherwise than in the course of a business to such an extent as to affect prejudicially the copyright owner

any device, product or component primarily designed, produced or adapted for the purpose of enabling or facilitating the circumvention of effective technological measures [i.e. chipping].

Section 296ZB(2) It is an offence to provide, promote, advertise or market a service to facilitate [the above]

(a) in the course of a business, or

(b) otherwise than in the course of a business to such an extent as to affect prejudicially the copyright owner.

Section 296ZB offences are hybrid offences for which a maximum sentence of 2 years' imprisonment and/or the statutory maximum fine are available by way of penalty on indictment.

Section 297 – Fraudulent reception of broadcasts e.g. satellite television programmes

Section 297(1) It is an offence if a person dishonestly receives a programme provided from the UK with intent to avoid payment.

Section 297(1) is a summary offence only, for which the maximum penalty is a fine not exceeding level 5 on the standard scale.

Section 297A – Unauthorised decoders

Section 297A (1) A person commits an offence if he:

(a) makes, imports, distributes, sells or lets for hire or offers or exposes for sale or hire any unauthorised decoder;

(b) has in his possession for commercial purposes any unauthorised decoder;

(c) instals, maintains or replaces for commercial purposes any unauthorised decoder;

(d) advertises any unauthorised decoder for sale or hire or otherwise promotes any unauthorised decoder by means of commercial communications.

Section 297A offences are hybrid offences for which a maximum sentence of 10 years' imprisonment and/or an unlimited fine are available by way of penalty on indictment.

Fraud Act 2006

The act creates an offence of fraud. Additionally, there are offences of making or possessing articles for use in or in connection with fraud, and making or supplying articles for use in fraud. Fraud can extend to the sale of counterfeit goods per se, and particularly if sold as genuine, or sold at the same price as the genuine product. In addition, the possession, use or sale of chipping or copying equipment could also give rise to offences contrary to the act.

Section 2 – Fraud by false representation

This offence requires dishonesty, intention to make a gain for oneself or another or an intention to cause loss to another or expose another to a risk of loss. Dishonesty is determined by the reasonable standards of honest people. The representation can be direct or implied, so a trade mark falsely applied to goods could constitute either a direct or implied representation as to the trade origin or manufacture of the goods.

Section 6 – Possession of any article(s) for use in the course of or in connection with any fraud

The defendant must have the article in his possession or control for use in, or in connection with fraud. Control here is less than possession – i.e. custody or access to the article if owned by someone else.

Section 7 – Making or supplying articles for use in fraud

The defendant must make, adapt, supply or offer to supply any article knowing that it is designed or adapted for use in the course of or in connection with fraud, or intending it to be used to commit, or assist in the commission of, fraud. This section could extend to counterfeit goods or the manufacture or supply of chipping or copying equipment.

14

How to develop your brand and grow your assets

Brand development

Your brand is the outside world's perception of your business. It is your company's identity and individuality. Your brand stands for your company's philosophies and beliefs as seen through the eyes of anyone who comes into contact with any of your business activities.

Drop all preconceptions that you have of branding before attempting to develop your own. A brand grows; it is not created overnight. You cannot suddenly ask the entire world to associate the words Coca-Cola with a brown, sweet, fizzy drink or the word *Nike* with sports gear and trainers – these perceptions have evolved over a number of years and with extensive advertising and marketing.

“ your brand is the outside world's perception of your business ”

Developing their brand is seen by some budding entrepreneurs as being of paramount importance. This is usually because they are too focused on what their competitors are doing and, as a result, not capitalising on their own strengths enough.

If you are in the position of being able to chuck a huge pot of money at marketing and advertising your new brand then by all means go ahead, but I cannot guarantee that you will get the results that you anticipate from such a spend. More likely than not, you will simply find yourself with empty pockets and a confused audience.

You need to adopt the creative approach to developing your brand and growing your assets. Recognise that, as with all development, this process is going to happen in cycles. Your brand will evolve. It will evolve steadily and surely with your guidance as your business grows. Do not be tempted into believing that you can simply create a successful brand overnight.

> **do not be tempted into believing that you can simply create a successful brand overnight**

Brand names and market perception

Wikipedia will tell you that a brand is a 'name or trade mark connected with a product or producer'. However, your brand is so much more than your company name, even if you have secured this as a trade mark, and although the name of your business is important, it is not of ultimate importance.

Are you using your name? If so, why? What does your name tell other people about your business, the unique selling points of the benefits that you offer to them, the end user? It may well be that your name is totally appropriate as a brand name for your company but there may also be a better alternative. Think about your idea and what it is that your company does and then consider how you would like other people to think of you and your business.

Innocent Drinks, for example, produce pure, untainted juice made from fresh, organic fruits. Their very name reflects their image and ethos. *Google's* name has also become synonymous with the company's activities. The way you say the word 'Goo-oogle', instantly conveys the idea of searching, ogling or looking for something in a fun and friendly environment. The dessert makers *Gu* have achieved similar status with their brand in a relatively short period of time. This simple two-letter word is enough to get your mouth watering and, once you've tasted their delicious gooey puddings, you are unlikely to forget the positive connotations associated with this brand.

Think about your brand name in relation to what it says about your brainwave and business. For instance, calling a sandwich shop any of the following;

- Succulent Sandwiches
- Quick Snacks
- Jeannette's Sandwich Shop

tells a person coming across such a business for the first time, what that business does. The different names also stimulate different mental images of how this particular business trades. 'Succulent Sandwiches' implies that these sandwiches are tasty, mouth-wateringly good – succulent and supreme. 'Quick Snacks', on the other hand, suggests that you are not going to have to wait very long, that you can pick up a quick bite to eat and be on your way. It implies nothing about the quality of what you are going to be 'snacking' on, just that you can assume you will get your meal fast.

'Jeannette's Sandwich Shop' suggests that Jeannette is behind this business. When you walk into the shop, you would expect to see Jeannette standing there smiling, ready to make your sandwich. The fact that she has put her name to her business implies that she is proud of what she is doing and so, by association, you would expect a more personal, homemade service. But, what if you don't know who Jeannette is? What if she had been involved in a press scandal or what if Jeannette didn't actually work in that particular shop? Would you be disappointed by Jeannette? I think that you might, and that you might wonder what else about this business is not quite living up to its name. Instantly, your association and feelings towards this brand change.

Consider what would happen if we called our fictitious sandwich shop by a completely random name. 'Subway' seems to have worked, so what if we were to call it 'Underground'? If you walked past a brand-new shop and saw the name 'Underground' hanging above the door, would you immediately assume that the shop sold sandwiches? Sure, you might be able to tell by looking through the window that this was what the shop sold, but would the name itself instantly imply sandwiches, a quick snack, or fast-food to you? The name itself does not tell you anything about what the business does. Not until millions of pounds have been spent on advertising and marketing, several franchise agreements have been structured and 'Underground' appears on your high street will you be aware of the services and products this company sells.

What I am trying to illustrate by way of example is that building a brand becomes a much harder job when you start to become ambiguous with your name or the message you are trying to deliver to your target market. Don't ask people to work hard understanding what your business does. Instead, **ask your audience to build your brand on your behalf.**

> **" ask your audience to build your brand on your behalf "**

Going back to the concept of a brand: a brand is the **outside world's perception of you**. It stands for what your customers and clients perceive your business to be and, by ensuring that you have a good relationship with these customers, you can begin to ensure that your brand evolves successfully.

Ask your customers what they think of your business and products. What has their experience of your business been like? What were their expectations and did your business, product or service live up to these? Ask for their opinions and use these to implement changes in and improvements to what you are doing already. Responding to your customers' needs by fulfilling their expectations of your business is the most solid way to build your brand's reputation.

Many business owners, marketing managers and advertising salespeople will have you believe that your brand is key to your advertising campaign – that you need a strong logo in order to be able to show it off in your advertisements. Trust me when I tell you that, from the point of view of a small business start-up, this is simply not true. Brand advertising only works when you have a massive and highly recognisable brand in the first place. Say 'Kodak' and people think of cameras; say 'BMW' and the association is cars; say 'McDonald's' and we all know what we're getting here; say 'the name of your invention or company' and, at this stage, most people are going to look at you blankly.

What difference will it make if you splash your brand name all over the local papers? Very little difference at all. Their reaction will still be blank. People will not recognise your brand until they have experienced what it has to offer and built a long and lasting relationship with you. Only when you have got millions of people interacting daily with your brand, sharing their experience of your brand with their friends and family, having their expectations met and fulfilled regularly and consistently on a massive scale will your brand reputation be of value. Until such a time, your brand is merely a communication tool in your bigger marketing plans.

❝ make it as simple and easy as possible for people to understand instantly what you do ❞

Make it as simple and easy as possible for people to understand instantly what you do. **Say what it does on the tin.** And, then start telling people about it.

Valuable assets

It is at this point that you can really start to develop not just your brand or your portfolio of products, services and intellectual property but the real assets of your business. Extracting wealth from your assets relies on you creating strong bonds and relationships between each of these valuable components. It is from within these bonds that you can build your assets and benefit from the healthy return on your investment that you truly deserve.

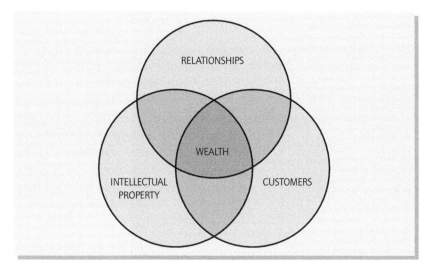

Your customer list

The most valuable asset in any business is the list of people who they are regularly selling to, followed by the list of people who have bought from them in the recent past and the list of people who could potentially buy from them in the near future. Your customers and clients are your business's most valuable asset; you need to be looking after them accordingly.

> **each person that comes in to contact with your business contributes to the reputation of your brand**

Remember: Growing your brand and the value of your business depends entirely on your customers. It is their feelings, opinions and willingness to spend money with you that counts. So building either your brand or your business successfully is going to mean building your most valuable asset: relationships with your customers.

Each person that comes into contact with your business contributes to the reputation of your brand.

They also have the potential to be worth £ (insert your average lifetime customer value) to your business. Ideally, you want to know **who they are, what their needs are and what their experience has been.** Only then can you really start to understand how best to build your brand.

Understanding your customers' needs will also give you a clear indication of how to grow your product and IP portfolio. Your first innovation was developed because you believed there was a need for such a solution in the marketplace. Now you can really begin to understand the problems that your customers face and grow your business and your product portfolio accordingly.

Negative news seems to travel 5 times faster than positive news. React to the negative news; you are bound to hear about it. Correct the problem so that it does not occur again and move forward, knowing that there is one less hole to plug. Thank people who point out negative news to you – it is only really through listening to this that we can take steps to make amends.

Marmite™ is a prime example of this. They understand that not everybody loves Marmite™; in fact, a large number of people actually hate Marmite™. They have taken this harsh critique of their product and turned it into a highly effective, very positive marketing campaign – so much so, indeed, that the term 'marmite' is now often used to describe something or someone you either love or hate. This is an extremely effective use of negative feedback.

Warren Buffett is also an advocate for this approach. In a speech he gave at the Emory Business School in Atlanta, Georgia, he expressed that he often felt that there was more to be gained from studying business failures than successes:

In my business, we try to study where people go astray and why things don't work. We try to avoid mistakes. If my job was to pick a group of 10 stocks in the Dow Jones average that would outperform the average itself, I would probably not start by picking the 10 best. Instead, I would try to pick the 10 or 15 worst performers and take them out of the sample and work with the residual. It's an inversion process. Albert Einstein said, 'Invert, always invert, in mathematics and physics,' and it's a very good idea in business, too. Start out with failure and then engineer its removal.

Just don't forget to listen out for the positive news too! When your customers thank you, ask them to elaborate. Ask them if they would mind you recording what they have just said and using it in your marketing material. Most people will be delighted. Now you can empower these individuals to become ambassadors for your cause. Feature their positive comments on your website, in your next promotion, in a press release or advertising campaign. People who have had positive experiences with your business can grow to become worthy members of your 'herd'. Stay in constant contact with them and encourage them to share their positive experiences with their friends. As they do so, yet more people will be attracted towards your business for positive reasons and the more people who are attracted, the more people they will, in turn, attract. This is the power of magnetic attraction – use this energy to drive people towards your business positively and productively. Build relationships with these new individuals and maintain live, long-term relationships with your early pioneers.

Your intellectual property portfolio

When you know who your customers and clients are, once you have worked really hard to understand their needs, responding to these needs becomes second nature and intrinsic to the growth of your business.

You know how to innovate and develop new products with strong features and benefits. Increasing your portfolio of intellectual property will increase the value of the assets in your business.

Keep your intellectual property portfolio up to date and your confidential trade secrets under wraps.

Concentrate on attracting and retaining long-term, loyal customers as satisfied and well-educated pioneers for your business and your brand and its reputation will take care of itself.

signposts for success

- If you would like help deciding what best to do with the **return on your investment** that your marketing is generating – turn to page 154.

- If you need to go back and better **plan your business** – turn to page 55.

- If you are ready to **refresh and refine your sales skills** – turn to page 101.

- If you would like to **generate some more ideas** and broaden your scope with a round of innovative expansion – turn to page 16.

chapter

15

How to manage and multiply your success

Celebrating success

Success should always be celebrated! If you remember, at the start of this book I mentioned that, in general terms, out of 33,000 ideas only one ever becomes a reality. By turning your brainwave into a business you have achieved just this. You have beaten odds of 33,000:1 and this is an absolutely fantastic achievement.

James Dyson's autobiography is called *Against the Odds*. It's a book worth reading but it is also an incredibly apt title. The success that this one man has experienced truly does come against all odds. You too should appreciate your tremendous achievement and celebrate your success. But, your adventure is far from over. The pitfalls just got bigger and the ground a lot less charted.

> **success is not a final destination; it is part of your continuing journey**

Certainly, it is important to celebrate your success. This is, after all, the whole purpose of setting a goal in the first place. Goals give you a clear measure of how well you are doing and celebrating achieving these is what will fuel your motivation and positively affirm your commitment to the process. Just remember one thing: success is not a final destination; it is part of your continuing journey.

Successful people are not born this way. They reach a point on their journey whereby they are able to live a successful and fulfilled life. This is why you need to be clear about your definition of success before you set out to achieve it. Time and time again, innovators and ideas people have misunderstood what success really means to them and died poor and dissatisfied as a result.

Roger Bacon, the inventor of the magnifying glass and a man with many novel ideas in respect of the development of aircraft was sentenced to prison by the Franciscans for 'novelties'. William Lee, the inventor of the stocking frame was refused a patent and died poor. John Hargreaves, the inventor of the spinning Jenny, had his idea stolen, his house attacked and his machine vandalised – he died a poor man. John Kay the inventor of the flying shuttle was also attacked, had his property vandalised and died poor. Charles Goodyear, the inventor of vulcanised rubber and the inspiration for the Goodyear Tyre Company died a poor man. John Harrison who invented the marine chronometer lived in poverty and spent years fighting the government for the prize money, only eventually to die a poor man. Nikola Tesla, an inventor who ended up with more than 800 patents to his name, including AC transformers, the fluorescent light bulb and the neon light, died in relative poverty. Sir Christopher Cockerill, the inventor of the hovercraft, never made any money from his invention. Even Thomas A. Edison died in relative poverty. The list goes on and on.

On the other hand, those who are clear about the goals they wish to achieve, focused on how they are going to achieve them and unambiguous about the measure of results that indicates when each goal has been scored, are much more likely to see and live the success that their efforts deserve.

Look at Bill Gates, Richard Branson, Steve Jobs, Anita Roddick or Alan Sugar. These aren't just people who had brilliant ideas. These are people who took measured and precise action to turn their ideas into brilliant businesses. The levels of success they celebrate are merely reflections of the dedicated effort and continued action they have taken to turn their brainwaves into the reality they initially aimed for. They have become masters of business, masters of marketing, masters of themselves and masters of motivating others. They have never once rested on their laurels, expecting success to land in their lap. Rather, upon achieving one goal, they have simply moved the posts and raised their performance. There is a lot to be learnt from studying such success models.

Shifting success

The truth is, the more you know, the more you realise how much more there is to learn. As Albert Einstein famously said:

As our circle of knowledge expands, so does the circumference of darkness surrounding it.

It is the same with success and goal setting. As we achieve our goals, goals that previously seemed out of reach begin to enter our field of vision. It is important that you realise that, although a goal might be something that you are striving for, once you have achieved it you will not necessarily feel satisfied sitting in the seat of success. Instead, if like most individuals who even begin to consider the prospect of turning their bright and burning brainwaves into brilliant businesses, you are a highly motivated and driven individual then, sitting in a seat (however comfortable or successful it may be) doing nothing all day will quickly leave you feeling uninspired, demotivated and saddened by what you originally perceived to be successful. Avoid leaving yourself in an empty vacuum upon achieving your goals but be prepared to move the goalposts and keep continually growing and striving for further targets.

> **be prepared to move the goalposts and keep continually growing and striving for further targets**

Sahar Hashemi, the founder of Coffee Republic and a woman who built her business from zero to £30 million openly talks about how empty, lonely and dissatisfied she felt when she sold her business for a small fortune. She achieved remarkable success but this did not give her personal satisfaction because she had failed to identify her next goals.

You are a person who enjoys action and therefore you have to keep taking it. No place called 'success' exists; it is an atmosphere that surrounds you as soon as you have aligned your reality with your hopes, dreams and aspirations. This is why it is important that you continue to shift the parameters of each achievable goal until you find yourself travelling in an environment whereby success surrounds you daily.

Don't be disillusioned by your definition of success. Be clear about what success means to you and plan how you intend to continually move through it as this is the only way to find a level of true and meaningful satisfaction.

Compounding success

Success can be multiplied. Not only can you achieve success but you can also achieve more of it. This is where people like Warren Buffet excel. Warren Buffet actively credits much of his success to his ability to compound it positively. Compounding interest (or compounding of earnings) is simply the

> **success can be multiplied**

ability to make more out of the return on your initial investment, thereby giving you more to invest further and more to make from this as a result.

In monetary terms, this is how it works. Say you were to deposit £1,000 in a bank or other financial institution and this earns interest for you at a rate of 5% which is payable annually. As the end of year one, you will have earned £50 and you will still have £1,000 in a bank. By reinvesting the interest as well as the original amount (£1,050), provided interest rates stay the same, the following year you will actually earn £52.50. If you reinvest this again, the year after that, your now £1,102.50 will actually earn you £55 and so on and so on.

This is the benefit of compounding. Naturally, the higher the interest rate, the higher your overall return will be. Warren Buffet is said to look at the compounding factor when deciding on investments by setting a requirement of at least 10% as a high probability of growth in earnings before he decides to make his initial investment.

This is worth considering. Observe your own success model. What has been the return on your own initial investment? Could you benefit from investing in similar projects in the future?

Supporting others

Support success

Giving to and supporting other people can be immensely satisfying in itself. There is no doubt that you will have learnt a vast amount on your journey of turning your brainwave into a successful business. Now is your chance to support and help others to achieve the same. Doing so could further compound your own success. As teachers, educators and facilitators, we always tend to learn more than those who we are actually teaching. So, by helping others, you could, in effect, be helping and supporting your own growth and further achievement.

Support society

As I write this, I am acutely aware of the global crisis that faces us. The world is facing huge problems – environmental, economic and social. It is my belief that innovation has got us into this mess and it is also my belief that innovation is going to get us out of it. People like you, who are striving to make a difference, are ultimately going to be the ones who provide us all with a better future.

Be clear about what success means to you. Celebrate it when you achieve it. Congratulate yourself on turning your brilliant brainwave into a successful start-up business! Continually grow and strive for further success by compounding what you have achieved already and look after yourself and others along the way.

It is an exciting and deeply rewarding journey. May you see limitless success, fruitful fulfilment and the rewards of reaping what you sow. I wish you all the best of luck on your way.

Useful contacts

UK

The British Inventors Society
Phone: 0208 547 2000
Website: www.thebis.org

The British Invention Show
Website: www.britishinventionshow.com

UK Department for Business, Innovation and Skills
Website: www.bis.gov.uk

The IP Crime Group
E-Mail: ipcrimegroup@ipo.gov.uk

The Anti-counterfeiting Group (ACG)
Phone: 01494 449 165
Website: www.a-cg.org

The Alliance Against IP Theft (AAIPT)
Phone: 0207 803 1234
Website: www.allianceagainstiptheft.co.uk

The British Music Recording Industry (BPI)
Phone: 0207 803 1344
Website: www.bpi.co.uk

The Entertainment Leisure Software Publishers
Association (ELSPA)
Phone: 0207 534 0580
Website: www.elspa.com

The Business Software Alliance (BSA)
Phone: 0207 245 0304/7340 6080
Website: www.bsa.org

The Federation Against Copyright Theft (FACT)
Phone: 0208 568 6646
Website: www.fact-uk.org.uk

PRS for Music
Website: www.prsformusic.com

The Federation Against Software Theft (FAST)
Phone: 0845 521 8630
Website: www.fastiis.org.uk

HM Revenue & Customs
Phone: 0845 010 8500
E-mail: ecustomer.support@hmrc.gsi.gov.uk

IFPI – The International Federation of the Phonographic Industry
Phone: 0207 878 7900
Website: www.ifpi.org

The Intellectual Property Office IP Crime Policy Team
E-mail: ipcrimeteam@ipo.gov.uk

International

For useful international contacts visit www.FromBrainwaveToBusiness.com

Seven reasons for you to thank my granny for making it possible for *you* to own this innovative and exclusive new cookware

This cookware was my granny's idea.

She noticed the problem and pointed this out to me. After all, I was supposed to be the hot-shot designer, wasn't I?

But really, all I did was come up with the answer to the question no one but my granny had ever thought to ask.

Let me explain … and bear with me. The detail is important.

Most of us struggle to lift a hot and heavy saucepan from time to time!

Especially my gran.

She loves cooking … but she found she was getting a terrible, painful, burning sensation starting in her wrist and forearm every time she tried to lift a heavy pan. So she'd grit her teeth and struggle, and have to reach forward to clutch the pan with two hands. But the harder she gripped the handle to stop the pan from tipping forwards, the more excruciating the pain became, shooting from her fingers to her elbows. It was always **a race between dropping the pan and getting it somewhere safe**. Needless to say, Granny didn't like this at all … and she didn't hesitate to let me know about it, either. But … guess what?

The more I thought about it and talked to friends and family and even professional chefs, the clearer it became almost **everyone** has this problem from time to time. And it's nothing to do with age, sex, size or strength. I know plenty of hunky men who secretly suffer too.

I call it the 'pain and strain of cooking' ... and by owning my pans ... you will eliminate it from YOUR kitchen!

The first thing you'll notice when you look at my pans is the handle. Yes, it's bent ... because bending is what causes the pain in your wrist.

So the simple solution no one has ever thought of before is: **bend the handle instead!** Eureka! That light-bulb moment!

Traditionally, saucepan handles have always been long and straight (which goes back to the days when we used to cook on fires at ground level and the long handle was essential to stop the cook burning themselves on the naked flames ... a bit of history for you).

Modern saucepans simply have a shorter version. And this straight handle forces you to bend your wrist awkwardly, reducing your grip by as much as 45%.

It also causes that awful **pain and strain** of cooking. Over time, it can develop into a nasty, chronic injury which causes kitchen misery for as many as 8 out of 10 professional chefs.

So simple, isn't it?

But it's more than just a bent handle.

You see, I spent **4 full years of my life** searching science journals, scouring libraries, burying myself in the internet and carrying out literally thousands of ergonomic tests and studies, picking the brains of doctors and surgeons to best understand the ergonomics of cookware.

And my range of pans is the result of that painstaking work.

Beautiful, yes?

The British Design Council has called this concept 'a watershed in cookware design' and the British Home Enhancement Trade Association has said that this is 'the biggest innovation to hit our industry since non-stick'. World-famous celebrity chef Ainsley Harriot said ... well, I can't repeat that here, but believe me it was very complimentary.

I've even won international design awards for it.

But the most important thing is **now you get to benefit, too**.

It's the first saucepan truly to be designed for use on a modern stove ... **and I guarantee you're going to love using it**.

If you are not completely convinced that this cookware is making your life in the kitchen safer and easier, if you are not totally satisfied with your investment then under the Doctor Cook Guarantee, just send your pans back to me, telling me why you are not completely happy with this pan and we will refit, replace or refund your investment.

It's not just about curved handles!

My granny (again!) insisted the pan be as feature-packed as possible and even the smallest milk pan had to have a 'proper' lid (she also insisted on superior-quality non-stick coating because this is her favourite pan).

So here are just some of the reasons you ought to thank my granny for this pan:

1. The soft-touch silicone coating not only feels smooth in your hand but it also stops your hand from slipping, protects you from the heat of the pan and stays cool during use. Simply grab the pan in your naturally strongest and most comfortable grip and you're cooking … safely and without strain.

2. Subtle design features such as the unique *Touch Recognition Steam Control and Straining System*™ (the dimples in the knob and holes in the lid) allow you to quickly and easily prepare healthy steam-cooked meals.

3. The etched measuring scale makes it really easy to accurately measure fluids straight into the pan and the hanging loop allows you to store it neatly away.

4. The quality of the stainless steel and the performance of the conductive base plate give you a rapid and even transfer of heat (and the whole creation looks really cute in your kitchen).

5. And because the handle is shorter it actually takes up less room in your cupboards and sticks out far less on the stove.

6. It saves on the washing up because you can easily strain away unwanted fluids with ease (and no need for a colander!).

7. It's so easy to wash and keep clean you'll wonder how you ever managed to do without it.

This isn't about being different just to be different and impressing your friends and neighbours with your funky new saucepans.

It's about **top-quality cookware feeling lighter** and easier to handle. It's about **saving your time and energy** by making your life safer, easier and ultimately better as a result.

And don't thank me. Thank my granny.

Visit www.doctorcookware.com to find out more.

Celia Gates
European Female Designer of the Year 2007

Index